Yesterday's California

RUSS LEADABRAND,
SHELLY LOWENKOPF & BRYCE PATTERSON

Yesterday's
CALIFORNIA

Seemann's Historic States Series No. 3

E. A. Seemann Publishing, Inc.
Miami, Florida

Many individuals have kindly supported the authors' task of collecting photographs for this book. Their invaluable help is gratefully acknowledged. All photographs without an abbreviated credit at the end of each caption come from the collection of co-author Russ Leadabrand of Pasadena; all others were contributed by the following:

AMPAS	Academy of Motion Picture Arts & Sciences, Hollywood	Northrop	Northrop Corp., Los Angeles
BA	Bank of America Archives, Los Angeles	NIT	Northrop Institute of Technology, Inglewood
Borax	U. S. Borax, Los Angeles	NPS	U. S. Dept. of the Interior—National Park Service, Washington, D. C.
Burmah	Burmah Oil & Gas Co., Houston, Texas		
Caltech	California Institute of Technology, Pasadena	PAM	Presidio Army Museum, San Francisco
CDPR	California Department of Parks & Recreation, Sacramento	PHS	Pasadena Historical Society
		PPD	Pasadena Police Department
CDPW	California Department of Public Works, Highway Division, Sacramento	Redwood	Redwood Empire Assoc., San Francisco
		Ronnie	Art Ronnie Collection, Los Angeles
CFBF	California Farm Bureau, Berkeley	Roses	Pasadena Tournament of Roses Association
CNG	California National Guard, Sacramento	SBCC	Santa Barbara Chamber of Commerce
CRB	City of Redondo Beach	SD Title	Title Insurance & Trust Co., San Diego
Douglas	Douglas Aircraft Co., Long Beach; McDonnell-Douglas Corp., Huntington Beach	SFCVB	San Francisco Convention & Visitors Bureau
		SOCC	Standard Oil Co. of California, San Francisco
Evans	Floyd Evans Collection, Pasadena	SPNB	Security Pacific National Bank, Los Angeles
Holly	Holly Sugar Corp., Colorado Springs, Colorado	SPTC	Southern Pacific Transportation Co., San Francisco
Kaiser	Kaiser Industries, Oakland	Stanford	Stanford University News & Publication Service
Kelly	Marylinn Kelly, Oknard		
KFI-LA	Radio KFI, Los Angeles	Sunkist	Sunkist Growers, Inc., Sherman Oaks
LADWP	Los Angeles Dept. of Water & Power	Times	Los Angeles Times
LAFD	Los Angeles Fire Department	UCB	University of California at Berkeley
LAHD	Los Angeles Harbor Department	UCLA	University of California at Los Angeles
LA Title	Title Insurance & Trust Co., Los Angeles	UOC	Union Oil Co., Los Angeles
Lockheed	Lockheed Aircraft Co., Burbank	UPRR	Union Pacific Railroad, Los Angeles
Locklear	Locklear Family Collection, from Locklear: The Man Who Walked on Wings, by Art Ronnie	USASC	United States Air Signal Corps
		USC	University of Southern California, Los Angeles
Lowie	Lowie Museum of Anthropology, University of California at Berkeley	USCG	United States Coast Guard
		USFS	United States Forest Service
MAFB	Mather Air Force Base	USN	United States Navy—Office of Information, Washington, D. C.
MPCC	Monterey Peninsula Chamber of Commerce & Visitors' & Convention Bureau	Wells Fargo	Wells Fargo Bank History Room, San Francisco
Myers	Mabel T. Myers Collection, Pacific Grove	WI	Wine Institute, San Francisco
NA	National Archives, Washington, D. C.	Winchester	Winchester Mystery House, San Jose
NAA	North America Aviation, Inc., El Segundo		

Library of Congress Cataloging in Publication Data

Leadabrand, Russ.
    Yesterday's California.

    (Seemann's historic States series ; no. 3)
    SUMMARY: Brief text and numerous historical
photographs, engravings, drawings, woodcuts, etc.,
trace California's history from first settlement to
the early 1950's.
    1. California--History--Pictorial works.
2. California--Description and travel--Views.
[1. California--History--Pictorial works. 2. Cal-
ifornia--Description and travel--Views] I. Lowenkopf, Shelly, joint author. II. Patterson, Bryce,
joint author. III. Title.
F862.L46   979.4'0022'2   75-14450
ISBN 0-912458-54-2

This book is dedicated to the ladies:
Lucie Leadabrand, Anne Lowenkopf, and Linda Patterson
with thanks to them for their support.

THIS FRENCH MAP OF 1656, one of the first known maps of California, shows the state as an island, as it was first thought to be. The error, persisting for many years, was simple to explain: Baja California, a long peninsula, is separated from the mainland of Mexico by the Sea of Cortez (the Gulf of California). Early explorers discovered pearls near the tip of Baja, but did not push all the way up the Sea of Cortez to discover that at its top was the mouth of the Colorado River. This map notes the visit of Drake and of the Spanish, and distorts the position of the offshore islands that run up the Pacific coast. The greater detail inland, in the Nuevo Mexico area, pays respect to the abortive attempts of Coronado to find the Seven Cities of Cibola, which were thought built of gold. This map contains enough information to cause any serious geographer or historian to thirst for more such cartographic anomalies. (LA Title)

Contents

Preface

THERE HAVE BEEN a long procession of picture books depicting all of California, or small pieces of California—historically, geographically, or whimsically. It would not be difficult to build a library on California, based on picture books alone.

I have labored over a couple of rather successful picture books before this one. It is an interesting book-making experience.

This one has a difference. It is based on a concept of Ernest Seemann of Miami, Florida, who has put together a successful series of photographic histories of places—cities and states—and his books have achieved a happy success.

Still, California *is* different. Here there are more things that have been photographed, there are more formal photographic collections which are widely scattered, and to which the keys are hidden variously.

To do this kind of picture book on California has been a curious and somewhat frustrating chore. Because any photophobe is bound to fall prey to the Pygmalion Trap: he is going to want to look for, find and use all of certain categories of photographs that he can.

I, personally, foundered in a sea of excellent historic aviation and dirigible pictures I uncovered. Next I discovered that there were too many delightful police photographs of the old days. Again, with effort, I was restrained.

The result, we all hope, is a satisfactory medley of historic photographs of the Golden State.

Some of the photos were simple to gather. Some came from my own rather extensive personal collection, put together over the past thirty-five years. Some photos were a battle to locate, and another to get prints of them.

This volume is not meant to be definitive on any level. To assume that such a book were possible would be the most incredible conceit. It would take a series of volumes, an unending procession of photo books, that would rival a five-foot shelf of any works.

It is then a medley, a sampler, a mood piece. California in microcosm. It is meant to be pleasant, and fun, and nostalgic, and provocative. California, one way or another seems to have gotten into everything in its young life.

This book could not have been assembled without some help from those outside our family. Those who contributed most mightily were Victor Plukas of the Los Angeles home office of the Security Pacific Bank's Historical Photographic Collection. Add Stuart Nixon in San Francisco, who pulled us through the rough patch in finding photos of the bay area. Delorez Nariman, historical librarian of the Title Insurance Company in Los Angeles, juggled her work load to accommodate our pressures and deadlines. List also Larry Booth, of Title Insurance, San Diego. And, of course, many more. But this is to be a picture book, not a list of old and new friends.

And, for a shot of bitters in the cocktail of old photos, we have decided not to avoid some of the old sources: history and tall-tale controversies. History is only just so precise. We have embraced some fine old-line prejudices and opinions. Don't credit them to us. We dug back a way to come up with this kind of spice. I hope none of California's giants, from Drake to William Randolph Hearst, think us less than respectful.

A medley, a sampler, a teaser, really, an appetiser. . . . For I am sure that Ernest See-mann will offer you, in good time, other picture books on this complex, slightly cockeyed, highly diverse, and controversial piece of real estate that the three of us have made our home . . . and love. Enjoy it just for what it is. Take away nor add anything. I, personally, had an armful of more pictures of flying wings and 1920s policemen. Shelly Lowenkopf and Bryce Patterson have let me do the talking here. I thank them and bid you sit and have some fun with us all.

Pasadena, July 1, 1975   Russ Leadabrand

Yesterday's California

IT TOOK a mere fifty years from Christopher Columbus' landing in the New World for Spanish conquistadors to cross Mexico, destroying at least the Aztec Empire in the process, and drop anchor in California's San Diego Bay.

The Spaniards came searching for riches as would future migrants to the West Coast of America.

Hernan Cortez started the chain of events that would lead to California settlement in 1532, when he ordered Diego Hurtado de Mendoza on the first "voyage of discovery" along the West Coast. The Spanish captain did not have an easy time. One of his ships returned to port almost immediately filled with mutinous sailors. The one ship that continued on the expedition was never heard from again.

Ships sent to find Mendoza failed, but returned reporting the existence of treasure islands. The fact that Indians killed more than twenty of the explorers was not enough to deter the Spaniards when treasure was available. They were so enamored with the area that Cortez named it California, after a popular tale about an island "very near to the Terrestrial Paradise," without ever seeing it. He ordered further exploration, and for some time California was thought to be an island.

By 1542, Juan Rodriguez Cabrillo dropped anchor in San Diego Bay and explored northward. Although he died as the result of an accident during the voyage, Cabrillo's party eventually made it north to Cape Mendocino, south of the present city of Eureka.

The Spaniards lost interest in their new territory when they became convinced it contained no riches, and offered no short cut to Europe. The only advantage they saw in the apparently impenetrable Pacific wall was the protection it offered to the galleons that for years brought the wealth of the Orient from Manila to Acapulco.

The British sea rover, Sir Francis Drake, breeched their wall in 1579, conquering South America's stormy Cape Horn, sailing up the Pacific Coast, and careening his ship, *The Golden Hind,* on a disputed beach between San Francisco Bay and Point Reyes. The English buccaneer named the land New Albion, and claimed the entire territory for England.

When rumors of Drake's visit reached Mexico, the Spanish government became interested in California again. More exploratory voyages were sent out. Moving into the area from interior Mexico, Father Eusebio Francisco Kino became the first priest in California in 1701, when he crossed the Colorado River near Yuma to preach to the Indians.

Spanish interest was spurred again in 1734, when there were reports that Russia was about to expand south from its Alaskan settlements. Within two decades, the French had been forced out of their North American holdings and started looking greedily toward California.

In 1769, Don Juan Perez sailed from San Jose del Cabo, Baja California, with the vanguard of a four-pronged "sacred expedition" to colonize California. He reached San Diego Bay on April 11, with a load of soldiers, two Franciscan priests, and the artisans necessary to establish a colony. The second ship of the expedition arrived nineteen days later with a crew so ill from scurvy they had to be helped ashore.

Up from Mexico, across the deserts came two land contingents of soldiers, settlers and cattle. The first column arrived in the San Diego Bay area after a fifty-four day march. The second, with expedition commander Don Gaspar de Portola and Father Junipero Serra, arrived on July 1. The first permanent settlement in California was founded.

In accordance with his royal mandate to "rediscover and people the bays of San Diego and Monterey," Portola spent only two weeks in the new colony before setting out to explore and establish more settlements. While he probed the land mass, Father Serra established Mission San Diego de Alcala, the first of twenty-one missions to be founded in upper California.

In 1770, Portola installed a military post (called a *presidio*) and a colony on Monterey Bay. Father Serra quickly founded Mission San Carlos de Monterey adjacent to the presidio.

As soon as he returned to San Diego, Governor Portola sailed for Mexico, complaining bitterly about the land he ruled and the colonization program. The balmy climate and sandy beaches of California apparently had none of the appeal for him that would attract future settlers.

But colonization continued. Expeditions gradually fanned out into the interior valleys. More presidios were founded with their attendant missions. By 1775, five missions were in operation along the coast and Captain Juan Bautista de Anza was exploring a land route from the California coast to Sonora, Mexico. A royal decree placed California's capital at Monterey.

The missions were the basis for colonization in the new territory. Each of these outposts had its own fields, cattle herd, and vegetable garden. The Franciscans who operated the upper California missions collected around their missions all of the Indians they could find. The neophytes, as they were called, tended the flocks and gardens, and were taught the skills necessary for them to build irrigation systems, weave fabric, and construct stone buildings—all necessary to sustain missions. In exchange for their labor, the Indians received the word of God.

Indians were legally tied to their missions. To the padres, the mission system was

MISSION SAN FRANCISCO de ASIS, or Mision de los Delores (Mission of the Sorrows, was dedicated in 1776, just five days before the signing of the Declaration of Independence. It had been founded by a Franciscian priest, Father Junipero Serra, on San Francisco Bay, but the settlers there soon found the land unsuitable for farming and moved southward to the rich Santa Clara Valley near what would become the city of San Jose. The four-foot thick stone and adobe walls of the mission were constructed over relics of St. Francis, the medals of five saints and a quantity of silver money. After fifty-seven years of independence, and proselytizing among the Indians and Mexicans, it declined when all the mission lands were secularized, and the slave-like existence of the Indians was ended.

undoubtedly just what the Indians needed. Rescued from their pagan, if free, existence, they became skilled artisans, and were converted to Christianity. Others, including some of the Indians, saw the system as a form of paternalistic slavery.

The first Indian rebellion against the mission system came on November 4, 1775. An estimated eight hundred Indians swooped down on the crude Mission San Diego, seizing and killing Father Luis Jaume and a carpenter.

The presidios were the second civilizing factor in California. Their tiny garrisons had little to do but chase an occasional runaway Indian and hunt the wild game in the mountains. They were usually ill equipped, poorly paid, undermanned, and inefficient. Still, they were focal points of government, and they attracted the settlers trekking into the colony.

In 1784, Rancho San Rafael, the first California land grant, was issued to Jose Maria Verdugo. It included parts of the present cities of Glendale and Burbank.

As colonization advanced, foreigners began taking interest in California. In 1786, French scientist Jean Francois Galaup de la Perouse paid a visit to the area. John Groehm (Graham) arrived in 1794 and was the first American to visit the future state. He died the day his ship docked at Monterey. The next year, English explorer Captain George Vancouver was added to the list of visitors.

The American vessel *Otter* reached Monterey in 1796, and laid a weak foundation for future relations between Yankee sea captains and the provincial government. Captain Ebenezer Dorr secretly landed ten men and a woman, stowaways from the British penal

MISSION SAN FERNANDO, founded twenty-two miles northwest of the Los Angeles pueblo on September 8, 1797, was for years the producer of food important to both Los Angeles and the presidio at Santa Barbara. By 1819, it had an Indian neophyte population of 1,080. Under the warm valley sun it produced mountains of grapes, wheat, and other grain crops, and wool for the Indian looms from more than 7,000 sheep. Indians attached to the mission tanned hides, and made shoes, saddles, and other equestrian trappings. With the Mexican war against Spain, secularization of the missions, and later, American supremacy in California, the mission declined, lost its lands and Indians, and ceased to be an important provider for the area. By the end of the Mexican revolution of 1810, Mission San Fernando held $400,000 in worthless vouchers for food and equipment confiscated by the Spanish army.

colony at Australia's Botany Bay. Spanish authorities were furious when they heard of it. They calmed down when the aliens proved to be useful artisans.

The Americans who came later did little to improve relàtions with California officials. In 1803, several crewmen of Captain William Shaler's vessel *Lelia Bird* were arrested by San Diego authorities for illegally trading furs to the Indians. The ship's company came to their rescue, and an artillery battle developed between the ship and the Spanish troops.

The nineteenth century brought increasing foreign curiousity about Spain's farflung territory. Despite efforts to discourage commerce between California and foreign nations, Spain was unable to keep its colony supplied with the goods needed for survival. The weak Mexico City administration was even unable to prevent Russian fur hunters from building Fort Ross in northern California in 1812. The weak presidio garrisons were at a loss to block British, French, South American, and American landings. The visiting vessels spread the news of the mild climate, the leisurely life-style, and the fertile, empty land throughout the world. Yankee sailor Thomas Doak became the first American settler in 1816.

Growing popularity also brought California its first and only pirate. In 1818, Hypolyte Bouchard sailed in and sacked Monterey, Refugio Rancho north of Santa Barbara, and an Indian village near San Juan Capistrano, before quitting the coast.

[14]

As soon as the first settlers began moving to California, a distinctive life-style started to emerge. Encouraged by a 1786 law that empowered the provincial governor to give large land grants and 2,000 head of cattle to each settler, ranchos became the basis of California society.

The land owners and their families toiled alongside their field hands, but their lives were relatively luxurious. Their adobe-brick houses, set in the midst of the ranches of fields and herds were plain but comfortable. They lived as part of the few truly self-sufficient, independent people in the world. The demands of the land, their isolation on the ranchos, and the slight importance of the fledgling provincial government left the ranchers free to ignore public affairs.

But growing international contacts, and the growth of a new generation of Californians who were more concerned with matters of state and political events within the crumbling Spanish empire would not permit the rancheros to maintain their sublime oblivion very long.

Mexico became independent in 1822, and residents of the province had to vote for representatives to the provincial assembly and the new imperial court. They were again called from their lethargy in 1824, when Emperor Iturbide's Mexican empire was crushed and Mexico became a republic.

This time, California was not so swift to get on the bandwagon. Instead of racing to join the republic, California officials adopted a plan for governing their province without the Mexican government.

About the same time, the attention of the rancheros was drawn to government by an Indian rebellion at the central California missions. Beginning at missions Santa Ines and La Purisima Concepcion, the revolt spread to Mission Santa Barbara, killing seven whites and twenty-five Indians before it was put down.

Shortly, the Mexican congress issued a decree promising security and land to foreign settlers. The only immigration restrictions were on foreigners holding land within twenty leagues of a foreign nation's border. The decree offered newcomers a square league of irrigable land, four leagues dependent on rainfall, or six leagues of grazing land, tax free for five years. It was an open invitation to an influx of new social and political ideas.

California joined the Mexican Republic in 1825. At the same time, Governor Jose Maria de Echeandia made a major change in the basis of California society when he started secularization of the missions.

Pressure against the mission system had been building for years as the rising generation of young Castilians decided the Indians were really slaves. At first, secularization only gave the Indians at San Diego, Santa Barbara, and Monterey the right to form towns and and hold land. It was strictly supervised and heavily regulated.

In 1833, however, the Mexican government ordered dispersion of all mission lands and herds to the Indians. The missions were converted into towns, the head of each neophyte family received land, mission land was set aside for villages, and half the mission herds were distributed to the neophytes.

The original plan called for the Indians to be barred from selling their land or goods,

PIO PICO, the last Mexican governor of California, and his wife Dona Nachita Alvarado de Pico with their nieces, Maraneta Alvarado, left, and Trinidad de la Guerro, on the right: Born at San Gabriel Mission in 1801, Pico fomented a revolt against the arrogant Governor Vittoria in 1831, and, with the assistance of his brother-in-law Jose Antonio Carrillo, took over as California's governor. In 1833, he signed the Secularization Act that stripped the missions of their wealth and lands and much of their control over the Indians. Then, through friends and purchases, he became one of the great land owners in the state, holding great sections that had belonged to missions San Gabriel, San Fernando, and San Juan Capistrano. The sixteen rooms of Pico's 33-room, two-story adobe that survived the 1870 flood, still stand in their setting of pepper, olive, and palm trees on the remains of the 8,000-acre ranch near Los Angeles that Pico used to refer to as his "little ranch." (LA Title)

a protection against their being robbed. Despite the law, California settlers helped themselves to the land and cattle. What land the Indians got was quickly purchased by settlers at low rates, and the Indians were soon penniless.

Throughout the period, the area was embroiled in political ferment. In 1829, disaffected soldiers rebelled, took control of the Monterey presidio, and were joined by other Mexican troops. The rebellion was soon put down, but two years later, Pio Pico, Juan Bandini, and Jose Antonio Carrillo led another rebellion that forced the abdication of Governor Manuel Victoria.

Eventually, General Jose Figueroa became governor. He soon died, Colonel Mariano Chico took office, and lasted a year before he had to flee. Nicolas Gutierrez took over just long enough to come under military attack by Don Juan Bautista Alvarado. Jose Castro, and an army of approximately one hundred Californians demanding the appointment of a province native to govern.

In 1836, the provincial legislature declared California independent from Mexico. The situation lasted until General Anastasio Bustamante, a candidate the Californians liked, became president of the Mexican Republic. Juan B. Alvarado became governor and served for six months before Don Carlos Carrillo took power. Carrillo stayed on until 1838, although Alvarado consistently contested his authority.

Throughout the era, immigrants continued to reach the province. Jedediah S. Smith and a group of American trappers were among the first white men to arrive overland from the United States in 1826. It was not until 1840, however, that the most important American settler reached San Francisco. John Augustus Sutter, a Swiss citizen born in the Grand Duchy of Baden, had lived several places in the United States and Hawaii before settling in California. His land grant gave him title to eleven leagues of land on the site of present-day Sacramento, and the right to build and fortify a stockade. He had total authority in his domain, short of starting an Indian war.

By 1841, the first overland immigrant train of thirty-two men, a woman, and a child reached California from the United States. It was the vanguard of many that would follow.

In addition to the new attitudes the settlers brought to California, they also developed a new commercial base for the province. Soon, American firms like McCullough & Hartnell took control of portions of the California economy.

At first, the rising tide of Americans in the settlements proved a conservative influence. Fearing that the Californians' efforts toward independence threatened their commerce, Americans backed the Mexican government.

The Spanish Californians, on the other hand, developed fears that the Americans' main goal was conquest of their territory. Their suspicions were confirmed in 1842, when U. S. Navy Commodore Thomas Ap Catesby Jones suddenly sailed into Monterey Bay and demanded the presidio's surrender. The commodore had sailed from his Peru base at the first rumor of the United States being at war with Mexico.

Within two days, the embarrassed American officer learned there was no war. He tore

AMERICAN SAILORS AND MARINES raise the flag over Yerba Buena on San Francisco Bay, July 9, 1846, early in the Mexican War. The insignificant village's Russian, American, and Mexican population had learned of the war's approach a few days earlier when an American adventurer, Col. John C. Fremont, slipped across the bay and spiked the guns of the dilapidated Castillo de San Joaquin, a fortress nearby. Their first warning of an American naval squadron off the coast, however, did not come until the guns of Capt. John B. Montgomery's ship U.S.S. *Portsmouth* fired a salute to the flag, jarring them from their breakfast tables. They found American troop formations filling the small square. Within three years, the tiny village changed its name to San Francisco and became world-famous as golf poured through it. (Wells Fargo)

up the surrender agreement and sailed away, leaving a note of apology for the provincial governor.

Commodore Jone's attack was little more than a blunder, but the message was not lost on Mexican residents. They were skittish of any American military official by the time Army Capt. John C. Fremont arrived in 1844 with a "scientific" expedition.

Fremont was well received by American Consul Thomas O. Larkin and Monterey Prefect Jose Castro until the Mexican official learned that two detachments of U. S. soldiers were camped on the countryside. The Americans were permitted to stay only after Fremont assured his host that his men were only interested in gathering scientific data.

Castro gave the Americans permission to winter in the province on the condition that they stay away from the coastal settlements. The U. S. commander agreed, and left Monterey to join his expedition.

Within six weeks, Castro learned that the Americans had moved into the Salinas Valley, his back door. He ordered Fremont out of California. In response, the American troops fortified Gabalan Peak, raised the American flag, and prepared for battle. They abandoned their fort and retreated when Castro marched out against them.

The American force withdrew up the Sacramento Valley, taking refuge with John Sutter for a time, and continued their retreat toward Oregon. En route, Fremont received secret dispatches from one Lt. A. N. Gillespie, who had been racing to catch the American forces. Although Fremont never divulged the contents of the dispatches, even during his court martial, he immediately halted his retreat.

It was not long before all of the American ranchers north of San Francisco received an anonymous paper warning that a group of Californians was on its way north to destroy American crops, cattle, and homes. The American settlers sought out Fremont for help, organized into a small band headed by Ezekiel Merrit, captured 250 horses bound for Castro's camp, and attacked the pueblo of Sonoma.

The June 14, 1846 battle for Sonoma was won without firing a shot. The rebels hauled down the Mexican flag and ran up a homemade banner of homespun with a stripe of red flannel along the bottom bearing the words "California Republic." The flag carried a brown star and a drawing of a grizzly bear.

In what would come to be called "The Bear Flag Rebellion," neither side was aware that the United States and Mexico had been at war since May 13.

Despite the capture of Sonoma and the growth of the civilian force to 130, with Fremont adding 72 mounted riflemen to their ranks, Mexican governor Pio Pico and General Castro were too busy with a private dispute to take action against the Americans. They were still in Los Angeles arguing when Commodore John D. Sloat became the second American naval officer to take Monterey. He again raised the flag over the presidio. This time he claimed the entire province for the United States. Two days later, the American flag flew over Sonoma and San Francisco.

The two Mexican officials finally recognized the threat and combined to resist the Americans. They raised 100 men and were waiting when a 350-man American force under Commodore Robert F. Stockton landed at San Pedro. But before a shot was fired, both Mexican leaders fled to Mexico. Los Angeles fell to the Americans.

COLTON HALL in Monterey, now a state museum, was where the constitution of California was written in 1849. In the political stampede that followed the Mexican War, Californians were anxious to enter the Union, but Congress was halted by the slavery question and delayed action admitting the new state. In their haste, the Westerners voted themselves into the Union without awaiting congressional action. (MPCC)

Some of the Spanish-Californian settlers later organized a group to attack the small garrison left in Los Angeles, but they were driven off when reinforcements arrived from San Francisco.

There were several other skirmishes with neither side having enough manpower or weapons to win a decisive battle until Col. Stephen W. Kearny reached the area on December 5, marching overland from Santa Fe. He destroyed Pio Pico's forces in the battles of San Gabriel and La Mesa early in 1847. The fight was so decisive that the Californians surrendered completely.

[19]

A FOREST OF MASTS covered San Francisco Bay in 1849 as ships filled with gold seekers came to anchor only to be immediately abandoned by passengers and crews alike in the throes of gold fever. (SPTC)

All the Americans required of their Mexican-Californian neighbors in the new U. S. territory was that they give up their heavy artillery and agree to abide by U. S. laws.

When the Mexican War ended in 1848, California became a part of the United States. The republic was not ready for the transition. No provision had been made for civil government in the territory, and an American congress, divided over the slavery issue was not prepared to face the question of admitting California to the Union.

Initially, the new territory was subject to Spanish, U. S. military, and U. S. civil law all at the same time. The military governor, Brig. Gen. Bennet Riley, finally tired of federal inaction and moved to settle the situation. He called a constitutional convention.

It met on October 10, 1849, and adopted a constitution that remained in force until 1879. An election was held for a governor, a lieutenant governor, and members of an assembly. The assembly met and chose John C. Fremont and William M. Gwinn to be their United States senators. General Riley immediately resigned, tacitly recognizing that California had joined the Union without congressional approval.

The move caused a bitter eight-month argument between pro- and anti-slavery forces in congress. On September 9, 1850, congressmen finally ratified California's action, admitting it to the Union as a non-slave state.

Since the first reports of California's mild climate and sprawling, fertile lands, free for the taking, had filtered back East, the influx of American immigrants had grown steadily. In the decade before California joined the Union, the trickle of migrants along the trails grew into a flood.

Across the Great Plains they came, facing hostile Indians and a merciless nature. Once across the broiling plains, the pilgrims climbed the Rockies, dragged themselves and their dying animals across the interior deserts only to face the almost impenetrable wall of the Sierra Nevada and the coastal ranges guarding their Shangri-La. Only the strongest survived. The weak were buried where they fell along side the trail.

There was no easy way to California. In the mountains, avalanches, cliffs, and snow storms were lurking. Of the eighty-one members of the Donner party that tried a shortcut through the mountains and were caught by the snows, only forty-five survived the winter of 1846-47.

Where mountain winters did not threaten, the torrid Imperial Valley, or the deserts and desert mountains lay in wait for the trekkers.

One group of approximately a hundred immigrants broke away from a wagon train headed from Salt Lake City to San Bernardino in 1849. They tried a shortcut to the gold fields, only to find themselves in what would later be known as Death Valley. Some members of the party made it across the valley and through the Panamint Mountains on the other side. Those with wagons soon found that they could not get through the mountains. The wagon-mounted pioneers broke into several groups. Most of them either abandoned their wagons and quit or went south around the barrier.

By the time the party had worked its way clear of the desert and arid mountains, fourteen had died, two whil struggling through the desert valley.

It was from this sort of hardship that California's treasure of legends developed. According to the legend of the Lost Gunsight, one of the Death Valley immigrants broke

SHIPS TURNED INTO BUILDINGS became common in the swiftly growing San Francisco of 1850. The city grew by leaps and bounds as wagon trains and ships arrived carrying hordes of gold seekers. Demands for building materials were beyond anything that could be met, but the bay was filled with ships whose crews had deserted to the diggings. With practically no public services available, including a fire department, much of the early city was destroyed by fires between 1851 and 1855.

the sight off his gun. He found a piece of silver float, carved himself a new sight, and continued on his way. Later, hundreds of prospectors prowled the Panamints looking for the "lost gunsight." It continues to lure treasure seekers into Death Valley.

Other settlers took ships to Panama, trekked across the steaming, disease-ridden, jungle-covered isthmus, and sailed up the coast to their destination.

This apparently massive migration shrank into insignificance, however, compared to the wave of humanity that broke over the state when James Wilson Marshall discovered gold in John Sutter's millrace.

Spilling out of ships and wagon trains, gold seekers overran the Spanish land-grant ranchos, ignoring the owners' titles. Businessmen and artisans abandoned their work and fled to the mountains looking for the precious metal. A single report of a gold strike was enough to completely empty a town in hours. Soldiers deserted, and so did the troops sent to get them back. Farmers left their fields untended, and San Francisco Bay was jammed with ships whose crews to a man went over the side as soon as the anchor found bottom.

Gold fever so infected the East that at one time there was an unbroken line of California-bound wagons strung from Missouri to Fort Laramie. A total of 17,000 persons had embarked from Eastern ports for the gold fields by March 1849. From 1847 to 1850, the state's population jumped from 15,000 to 92,497; by 1860, the population was 379.994.

San Francisco was the funnel through which most of this deluge of people came. The insignificant little bay-side port of Yerba Buena had grown slowly. Its most important

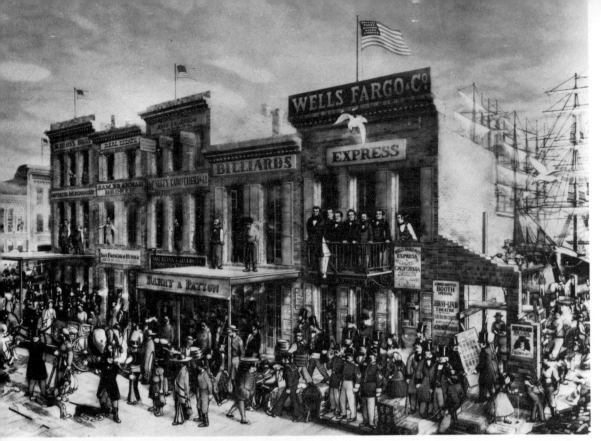

SAN FRANCISCO'S WESTERN WALL STREET grew up along Montgomery Street during the early 1850s. On the heels of the Gold Rush, banks began blossoming to handle all the newly found wealth. Surrounded by what was still essentially a wilderness and cut off by poor transportation, bankers in San Francisco did business like few others in the world. American money was so scarce that English shillings, French francs, Mexican double-reales, Peruvian doubloons, Spanish pesetas, Austrian zwanzigers, Dutch florins, and Indian rupees were often accepted. A pinch of gold dust substituted for a dollar. The term "two bits" evolved here when gold wire was drawn into lengths worth a dollar and notched into eight parts to be broken up for change. Before the U. S. Mint was established in the city in 1854, many of the banking and express companies had resorted to coining their own money. (Wells Fargo)

WELLS, FARGO & CO.'S first office in California was opened in 1852 on San Francisco's Montgomery Street—known as the Wall Street of the West—to move the gold flowing out of the mountain mining camps. The banking and express firm was one of the few survivors of the financial panic of the mid-1850s, but its building was destroyed in the earthquake and fire of 1906. Wells Fargo scales measured millions of dollars in gold in camps throughout the diggings before the rush was over. They are still on display in many of the more famous mining camps. Here, the first Wells Fargo staff poses for a daguerreotype in front of their new office. (Wells Fargo)

economic base before the discovery of gold was serving the cargo and whaling vessels putting in from the Pacific.

The city had thirty families in 1841; by 1846 it had grown to between fifty and sixty families; by the 1850s, 50,000 persons inhabited the sprawling, raucous town. It offered the lustiest entertainment available to the veterans of nine months around Cape Horn or the long trek across country. The roullette wheel of the Barbary Coast gambling halls was the town's coat of arms. Residents gambled in all sorts of commodities and real estate as well as at the gambling tables.

Up in the mining camps—Git-Up-And-Get, Bogus, Thunder, Angel's Camp, You Bet, Shinbone Creek, Red Dog, and Lazy Man's Canyon—the miner's kept crime under control. Committees would not tolerate flagrant criminal acts. Banishment from the camp and a long rope with a loop-end were effective peace-keeping weapons.

In San Francisco and Sacramento (built on the ruins of John Sutter's 97,648-acre domain, after it had been overrun by gold seekers), on the other hand, the influx of people from all over the world defied all control.

Lawlessness was common: Beatings, murder, robbery, and shanghaing became the norm This came to a head July 15, 1849, when the "Regulators" raided the Chilean quarter of San Francisco. This band of men were originally hired to recover runaway sailors. They soon turned into a fancy uniformed band of self-styled peace keepers called "Hounds" by the local residents. They considered it their mission to keep the city free of all foreigners to save it for white Americans.

The more stable residents had already grown furious at the glee the Hounds got from harrassing foreigners in the city. When a woman was murdered in the Chilean-quarter, and local officials were helpless, shop-keepers and bussinessmen formed their own mob, ran down nineteen Hounds, indicted them in a kangaroo court, and ordered their banishment. The Hounds were disbanded, but so was the band that had ended their reign of terror. Lawlessness still flourished.

[23]

GLAMOROUS ENTERTAINER LOLA MONTEZ joined Junius Brutus Booth, his son Edwin, Jenny Lind, Lotta Crabtree, and other famous entertainers in satisfying the Forty-niners' insatiable desire for entertainment and culture. A favorite of the San Francisco Fire Engine companies, she electrified her 1854 audiences with her famous Spider Dance, and became such a favorite in the mining camps that the miners named two lakes and a mountain in her honor.
(Wells Fargo)

WILLIAM T. COLEMAN was one of California's pioneer merchants, and an exponent of law and order in lawless San Francisco. He was a member of the city's first vigilance committee in 1851, and one of the main organizers of the second vigilance committee formed in 1856, serving as chairman of the organization. When Francis Marion "Borax" Smith started development of the borax deposits in Teel's Marsh, Coleman & Company became his marketing agent. When Aaron Winters found borax in Death Valley, Coleman built the Harmony Borax Works. He later bought the borax strike at Amargosa, not far from Harmony. With rich claims 165 miles from the nearest railroad, Coleman accepted Harmony Superintendent John W. S. Perry's idea for the mule wagons. His borax processing plant in Alameda, on San Francisco Bay, was just going into production when Coleman & Co. was forced into bankruptcy in 1888. It was with Smith's purchase in 1890 of the Alameda plant and the undeveloped borax properties of Coleman owned at Borate, that the Pacific Coast Borax Co. was formed. The firm later became U. S. Borax. (Borax)

SAN FRANCISCO VIGILANCE COMMITtee membership was marked by an ornate certificate after the second of the city's two vigilante groups was formed in 1856. The so-called "Lawless" bands formed in response to conditions that saw 1,000 murders in the city from 1849 to 1856, and a corrupt city government capable of a single execution in the same period. The committee grew so strong that state militia were incapable of taking over its power or gaining control of Fort Gunnybags, the vigilante headquarters. By the time it voluntarily disbanded on August 18, 1856, it numbered 9,000 members organized into infantry, cavalry, and artillery units. (Wells Fargo)

In 1851, the first San Francisco Vigilance Committee, made up of solid citizens, was organized under the leadership of a backsliding Mormon, Sam Brannan. The Vigilantes quickly took over enforcing the laws, showing a willingness to hang criminals no matter how petty their offenses. Within thirty days, the 100-a-month murder rate dropped off sharply. The Vigilantes disbanded.

In 1856, the second Vigilance Committee was formed when an influx of furloughed Australian convicts known as Sidney Ducks and of miners drifting in from played-out mines started another crime wave. The organization was so strong that the militia failed in an attempt to disband it by force. It disbanded on its own within a year as the crime wave subsided.

While the northern portion of California was exploding, the southern areas remained relatively quiet. The discovery of gold in the north at first drew people out of the Los Angeles area. The ones who remained on the farms and ranches that occupied the southern parts of the state soon found the gold rush was valuable even to them. Before the strike, the only products they'd had of any value were hides and tallow. Now, the gold camps demanded fresh meat. Small citrus-orchard and grape-vineyard operators faced a market that permitted almost limitless expansion.

During the 1850s and 1860s, Los Angeles gained a reputation as a tough town. Added to its own crop of rough characters, the town was a catch basin for the worst toughs run out of San Francisco and the gold camps. With a population of less than 9,000 in 1850, the town had an average of a murder a day. It did not count the Indians who were killed.

There were only 295 American Angelenos in 1850, but their slight numbers did not keep them from acting like their northern cousins. The favorite pastime was duping Mexican residents out of their land grants.

Gradually, the Southern California city developed light industry. Construction of a flour mill and a brick kiln was an important addition to the city's economy.

San Diego, destined to become one of the major urban centers of the state, remained a small village throughout the ferment of the mid-nineteenth century. It too had a reputation as a tough town, with badmen filtering down from the north, mixing with bandits driven out of Mexico. In one of the daily shooting scrapes, Roy Bean, the brother of San Diego's first American mayor, was arrested after a gun battle in which his fleeing opponent was shot in the back. Bean was arrested, but tunneled under the wall of his jail cell, escaping to Texas where he appointed himself judge and "The Law West of The Pecos."

Both southern cities needed transportation and adequate water before they could grow.

In 1854, the Northern California boom came to an abrupt halt, and financial empires suddenly collapsed. Unemployed miners filtered in from the played-out diggings, while wagon trains and ships kept bringing in new waves of gold rushers. The economic structure of the most-populated region of the state was coming apart, and the rootless newcomers began settling on the lands held by Spanish-American residents. Land companies hired professional squatters to take over the land, and corrupt politicians supported their claims.

The period from the mid-1850s to the Civil War was a time of retrenchment. Banks that had crashed during the slump were reorganized and reopened. Investment moved into real estate and other profitable ventures. The discovery of the Comstock Lode in Nevada attracted former California gold investments.

The decline in the mines and the massive unemployment was reflected in Southern California. The bottom dropped out of the farm and ranch products market.

As the Civil War approached, various political factions that came to California in the gold rush, started organizing and choosing sides. Northern California was basically anti-slavery and pro-Union. Southern California and most of the Democratic party in the state were pro-South.

In 1855, the Know-Nothing, or American, political party and secret society held its first state convention. The anti-Chinese, anti-Catholic organization nominated John Neely Johnson for governor. He was elected in 1856.

The widely divergent political views held by different segments of the state's population led to increased unrest. Settlers in the Honey Lake Valley of northeastern California held a mass meeting in 1856 and declared their independence from the state. The movement, under the leadership of Peter Lassen and Isaac Roop, quickly fell apart.

The far-western state was brought closer to the Union in 1858, when the Butterfield Overland Mail opened a western terminal in San Francisco. The improved communications with the East went a long step toward ending the fears on both sides of the continent that California would soon tire of its weak ties with the republic and declare itself an independent nation. Even U. S. Sen. William M. Gwinn warned that his native state would declare itself independent if the South seceded from the Union.

When news that war had broken out reached California, Southern sympathizers strove hard to carry the state into the Confederacy, or to keep it out of the conflict altogether. The legislature voted to stay in the Union on the urgings of the Rev. Thomas Starr King.

In spite of spying, the formation of secret societies, and grumbling from the pro-Southern press of Los Angeles, the gold of California flowed uninterrupted into the Union coffers throughout the war. On call from President Lincoln, the state even raised a regiment of volunteers for Union service.

More important to Southern California than the war was the drought of 1862 to 1864. When the rains failed to come, thousands of cattle and sheep died. Ranchers slaughtered their horse herds to preserve the little pasture available for the cattle.

The Civil War brought passage of the law providing for construction of a transcontinental railroad. The government was so worried about securing California that it gave the railroad builders free right-of-way, all the necessary stone, timber, and earth to do this work, and five alternate sections of land along each mile of the roadbed, just to make sure they would do the job. The government also agreed to give the builders $16,000 in government bonds for every mile of road they built. Six months before the bill was signed, Leland Stanford, Collis P. Huntington, Mark Hopkins, James Benley, and T. D. Judah had organized the Central Pacific Railroad Company of California to build a railroad from California east. The rails of the Union Pacific and Central Pacific railroads met at Promontory Point, Utah, on May 10, 1869.

SACRAMENTO IN THE 1850s was the supply center for prospectors in the northern mines of the Mother Lode. Lying in the loop of the Sacramento River at its confluence with the American River, the town was originally a part of the Mexican land grant to John Sutter. When gold was discovered, miners overran Sutter's baronial estate, stole his cattle, and drove off his Indian retainers. His white workers deserted him for the goldfields, and Sutter was pushed off the land. The town, growing quickly as saloons, fandango houses, and gambling dens took the gold of the miners, offered $1,000,000 in 1849 for the honor of being the state capital. The legislature first met there in 1852, immediately after a fire that wiped out two-thirds of the town. Before Sacramento became the official capital in 1854, three destructive floods tore through it. Epidemics were so rampant that the dead were merely rolled into the river to float away. In 1856, the city became the terminus of the first railroad in the state, a short line to Folsom. It was later the end of the transcontinental railroad.

[27]

WESTERN WRITER BRET HARTE got his start to world fame as the controversial editor of an Arcata newspaper in the 1850s. (Redwood)

JOAQUIN MURIETTA, California's most notorious bandit and killer, launched his career of crime following brutal treatment from a group of Yankee miners. He started as a crusader to rid his native land of what he saw as invaders, but ended up a common bandit. He is said to have eventually killed all the men that mistreated him, and ran up a total murder score of twenty-four to twenty-nine. Despite legends of his desire to regain the land for the Mexicans, most of his victims were Mexican ranchers or Chinese laborers. Capt. Harry Love and a posse of twenty rangers caught up with him in 1853, and Murietta and his lieutenant, Three-fingered Jack, were killed in the Priest Valley gunbattle. Bill Byrnes, one of Murietta's partners in a monte game, cut off the bandit's head, packed it in salt, and shipped it to San Jose. It and Three-fingered Jack's hand were put into alcohol and exibited throughout the state until they disappeared in the 1906 San Francisco earthquake and fire. (LA Title)

Although Californians had not been materially involved in the slavery question that precipitated the Civil War, the state had its racial problems.

Ever since the Gold Rush, resentment had been building against the Chinese and Japanese who were attracted to California by the promise of prosperity. Most of them stayed out of the gold fields. They migrated to the cities where they established small shops or worked at laboring jobs abandoned by the whites.

They were frugal, they demanded little, and they worked hard without being watched. Their willingness sometimes drove down salaries. On their heels came political movements designed to get them out of the state in order to eliminate them from competition in the labor market.

These movements remained small as long as the Oriental population remained small. When construction started on the transcontinental railroad, company officials could not find white workers willing to undergo the hardships and low pay of mountain rail construction. They imported thousands of Chinese workers on labor contracts.

TIBURCIO VASQUEZ, second only to Joaquin Murietta among California bandits, started his criminal career at the age of fifteen by stabbing a constable at a Monterey celebration in 1854. He escaped and was soon riding with a gang of horse thieves. In short order, the young bandit was mounted on a cream white charger leading his own gang in a series of robberies, and murders. Although his men never divided more than $2,000 between them, Vasquez was a thorn in the side of law enforcement officials because they could not catch him. His last raid in 1873 at Paicines left three men dead. He was captured, brought back to San Jose, and hanged in 1875. He became famous during his trial and hanging for maintaining a quiet dignity.

The assumption was that when their contract expired, or the job was done, the coolies would go back to China. Many did, but more moved into Northern California cities to look for work or to start their own businesses. They glutted the labor market, depressed salaries, and created lasting hostilities within the state's labor and political movements.

In 1871, a mob of 500 whites invaded Los Angeles' Chinatown looking for a notorious Chinese criminal. When they could not find him, they lynched eighteen innocent Chinese and looted the district. Six years later, an anti-Chinese riot in San Francisco resulted in the burning of a Chinese laundry, the destruction of several other Chinese businesses and the revitalization of the vigilance committee to preserve order. The continuing unemployment and Chinese competition in the labor market resulted in formation of the Workingmen's party, which demanded exile for Chinese workers, partition of large land holdings, and the transfer of government from the capitalists to the people. Its agitation led to several riots.

With the transcontinental railroad came new immigrants, adding pressure to the depressed labor market. Speculation in all sorts of wildcat mining schemes and oil ventures made and broke fortunes overnight.

A complex of financial maneuvers involving control of Nevada's Comstock Lode Bonanza mines resulted in the Bank of California's collapse. The entire state spun deeper into the slump. The cities were the scenes of bank panics. The farms and ranches, already burdened with high freight rates, land monopolies, and railroad-controlled water suffered a severe drought.

Out of the turmoil came a new state constitution giving more power to the people, and weakening the hold of railroad magnates and bankers on the government. It also barred the Chinese from voting, and led to state exclusion laws as well as California-led efforts to pass a nationwide Oriental exclusion law.

In the same period, the state had its one and only full-scale Indian war. There had been periodic Indian trouble since the area's days as a Spanish colony. But most of the incidents amounted to little more than local skirmishes. During the rush to the mountains for gold, miners had attempted to drive out or exterminate whole tribes. In 1872, soldiers and volunteers moved out to capture Capt. Jack Kientepoos after his band of Modoc Indians killed the members of an immigrant train and started raiding settlements. The troopers chased the Indians all over the rugged Lava Beds country of northeastern California. They came back exhausted, empty-handed, and lost several troopers in the effort. An army of a thousand men moved out after the tiny Indian band; they still could not catch the Indians in the labyrinth of canyons.

Efforts to make peace with Captain Jack failed, and the Rev. Eleazer Thomas, Gen. E. R. S. Canby, and a third man were killed in a later attempt. The furious soldiers then surrounded the band, captured the Indian leader and his lieutenants, brought them before a field court-martial, and hanged them. The remaining 153 members of the band were exiled to the Quaw-Paw Agency in Indian Territory.

THEODORE DEHONE JUDAH, a civil engineer, came to California at the age of twenty-eight to become chief engineer for the Sacramento Valley Railroad. Following a visit to Washington as a delegate to the Pacific Railway Convention, however, he announced that he had found a practical route through the Sierra Nevada mountains. Through his urging, Sacramento merchants Leland Stanford, Charles Croker, Collis Huntington, and Mark Hopkins formed the Central Pacific Railroad Company to drive the transcontinental rails east, from the coast. Judah, the new railroad's chief engineer, died in 1863, before any part of the system he inspired was put into operation. (SPTC)

THE FIRST RAILROAD west of the rockies began with the trial run of the Sacramento Valley Railroad on August 17, 1855. The twenty-two-mile line from Sacramento to Folsom speeded movement to and from the goldfields. (SPTC)

THE STEAMSHIP *Sonora,* one of the Pacific Mail Steamship Company's ships plying the Pacific coast from Panama to California ports, carried mail, passengers, and cargo that had made the difficult trek across the Isthmus of Panama to the growing communities along the California coast. It became famous in 1854, making an 11-day, 21-hour record run from Panama to San Francisco. (Wells Fargo)

While Northern Californians settled into a pattern of small towns, farms, and a few cities, Southern California remained a relatively under-populated area of tough towns among ranches and citrus orchards.

In 1869-70, San Diego experienced a gold rush of its own when rancher Fred Coleman found the precious metal in the Cuyamaca Mountains. San Diego, San Juan Capistrano, and San Bernardino quickly lost their populations as everyone went "to see the elephant." Mining camps—Mount Vernon, Julian, Banner City, Cuyamaca City, and Branson City— appeared from nowhere as prospectors burrowed into the hillside.

These gold strikes, however, did not produce the easy wealth of the earlier northern strikes. In San Diego, they were locked in seams forced up from deep within the earth when the mountains were made. This complex faulting meant that miners might be following a rich vein one day and be facing a blank wall of rock the next.

The geological situation put a damper on the gold rush and kept San Diego from undergoing the sort of boom that had earlier engulfed San Francisco.

Northern California's wild and wooly days had subsided, meanwhile, but from the mountains came another treasure, timber. The mountains and valleys of Northern California were covered with virgin timber, some of it the biggest trees in the world, the Sequoia redwoods.

Beginning in the 1880s and continuing until World War I, fortunes were made as the giant trees and their smaller cousins were stripped from the slopes and out of the mountain basins.

THE STEAMBOAT *EXPLORER* was used by War Department Lt. Joseph C. Ives in 1858 to explore the Colorado River. After traversing the river up to the mouth of Black Canyon, he wrote, "The region last explored is of course valueless. It can be approached only from the south, and after entering it there is nothing to do but return. Ours was the first and doubtless will be the last to visit this profitless locality. It seems intended by nature that the Colorado River (the Grand Canyon portion) along the greater part of its lonely and majestic way, shall be forever unvisited and undisturbed."

[32]

THE FIRST BAPTIST Church founded in Southern California was established in El Monte in 1853. The church also served as the hall for Lexington Masonic Lodge No.104. (LA Title)

SOUTH FARALLON ISLAND LIGHTHOUSE AND LANDING COVE, twenty-three miles off the Golden Gate: The islands, nothing more than a collection of jutting rocks, were known to the Spanish along the California coast in the sixteenth century, and to Sir Francis Drake, whose men gathered bird eggs and seal meat from the wildlife there. In 1819, Russian sailors started exploitation of the seals, collecting 30,000 skins in five months. During the gold rush, egg pickers battled with everything from fists to guns in their efforts to get the valuable eggs, and despite the islands having a reputation as a ship killer, the avid egg gatherers attempted to block construction of the Farallon light in 1855. Bricks for the construction were hauled up the winding trail to the top of the 358-foot crag a few at a time. When completed, the tower was found too small to fit the lantern and had to be rebuilt. Its 500,000-candlepower light shines twenty-six miles out to sea today as a warning to mariners. The islands have been a wildlife sanctuary since 1909. (USCG)

In 1876, the Southern Pacific Railroad drove its first line south into Los Angeles; but rails to San Diego would wait still longer, until there was some reason to bring them to the small village.

The growth of the areas that were to become the symbol of California urbanization and of the smog and sprawl that would plague the state a hundred years later did not come until the middle of the 1800s.

The massive rush of people to Southern California was brought about by a combination of spreading reports of the ideal climate, the fertile soil, the interest of Easterners in an exotic orange fruit, increasing popularity of California wine, and a rate war between the railroads.

The Southern Pacific had been doing a good business from the Midwest to Los Angeles at fares of $125 one way. The Santa Fe completed its line to the city in 1886, and started cutting rates. Fares dropped to $5, and soon to $1. Thousands climbed aboard, headed for their South Seas paradise in response to the touting of land speculators.

Land prices went from $500 a lot in Los Angeles to $5,000. Outlying areas, formerly worth $350 an acre, were surveyed and sold for $10,000 an acre. Hotels went up on empty deserts, and sidewalks ran past clumps of sagebrush where towns were expected to burgeon.

Corrupt land dealers sold vast stretches of coastline with claims that the water was always calm. They sold land covered with thorny Joshua trees for orange groves by sticking oranges on the thorns. Bands and "tallyho" carriages took prospective buyers to and from the land that would "surely" make them the ideal home and rich at the same time.

San Diego civic leaders saw the boom as a chance to take the important place in the state they had always felt they deserved. They were tired of being the butt of Los Angeles and San Francisco newspaper jokes, and they were still smarting from the humiliation of seeing their town go bankrupt, have its charter revoked, and be placed in the hands of legislature-appointed trustees.

San Diego speculators started buying land, subdividing, and advertising. Soon they were predicting a population of from 25,000 to 50,000 within five years. They pointed out that the transcontinental railroad was headed toward the city, that the Colorado River barrier to the east could now be crossed, and the interior Imperial Valley was rapidly developing into an agricultural empire.

The boom lasted only two years. The bubble burst in a flurry of collapsing banks, syndicates, and individual fortunes. San Diego lost half its 35,000 population in what seemed like no time at all. Los Angeles' population dropped to 50,000. Everywhere there were subdivisions that never got started, hotels sitting alone in the desert brush, and embryonic communities that would have to wait for a better day before they met the expectations of their transplanted residents.

[34]

A CHINESE JUNK flotilla of seven vessels rides at anchor in San Diego Bay around 1854. (SD Title)

AN ARMY CAMP IN NORTHERN CALIFORNIA on the trail of the elusive Modoc Indians: Although the more spectacular battles with the Plains Indians later captured the attention of the nation, the Army's pursuit of the Modocs was the nations's most expensive Indian campaign. The conflict started with white encroachment on Modoc land and an 1852 counterattack that killed sixty-five whites. In retaliation, the whites killed forty-one Modocs. The skirmishes continued until 1872, when the Indians surrendered and were deported to Indian Territory. (NA)

WARM SPRINGS INDIAN SCOUTS of the Modoc War pose for a government photographer. The scouts made it possible for the army units to keep up with the Indians as they fled through the rugged terrain of Northern California. (NA)

THE ALVARADO GUARD, shown here in 1864, was one of the many volunteer California militia units raised during the Civil War. (CNG)

ONE DAY'S RUN at the Cerro Gordo Smelter: After Mexican prospectors found silver on the western slopes of Buena Vista Peak in 1865, the desert town of Cerro Gordo became the greatest silver and lead producer in the history of California. The production of its two smelters was so prodigious that the thirty-two freight wagons in operation could not haul it all away. The twelve-mule teams had to make a dangerous descent down the mountain and then tramp a three-week course around Owens Lake. Later, the *Bessie Brady,* a steam paddle-wheeler, took the ingots across the lake to save time, carrying seventy tons of silver a trip. Since not enough wagons were available to haul it from the dock, by 1873, eighteen thousand silver bars ($600,000 worth) were stacked at Cartago, or used as bricks to construct winter cabins by some of the inhabitants. In 1879, the mines played out and the town disappeared, but before its demise it had produced $17,000,000 in silver and lead.

[36]

THE CENTRAL PACIFIC TRAIL through the Palisades is discovered here by an Indian in 1868 when it was constructed by approximately 65,000 Chinese laborers and American foremen. They built trestles, cut roadbeds, and drove tunnels at the rate of 1.18 feet per day through the granite mountain ranges that stand side by side across California. Six years in construction, and overcoming snows up to thirty feet deep in the Sierra winters, the Central Pacific has been designated a National Civil Engineering landmark by the American Society of Civil Engineers. (SPTC)

THE BIG FOUR who formed the Central Pacific Railroad: Groder Leland Stanford *(above, left)* later became governor and U. S. senator from California and founded Stanford University. Charles Croker *(above, right),* a dry-goods dealer, later began purchasing banks, forming one of the state's most important banking establishments. He was one of the state's early patron of the arts. Mark Hopkins *(below, left),* a partner in a hardware business with Collis Huntington, is remembered for the San Francisco Hotel that bears his name and occupies the spot where his mansion once stood. C. P. Huntington *(below, right)* later was a heavy contributor to San Francisco's Golden Gate Park. The four, starting with a total of $50,000, became financiers of major importance in the state and through the nation. (SPTC)

CHINESE RAILROAD BUILDERS of the Central Pacific survey one of many trestles they constructed across the Sierra Nevada and the other coastal mountain ranges to join the Central and Union Pacific rails at Promontory Point, Utah. The stoic little workers were first hired when the Central Pacific could not get enough Caucasians to do the job. Preferred for their dogged determination, they were paid the same as American laborers but did not demand as many creature comforts. When the railroad was finished, their release from work created a racial, political, and economic problem that plagued California well into the twentieth century. (SPTC)

[39]

CHINESE COOLIES WITH TWO-WHEELED carts laboriously fill the roadbed for the Central Pacific right-of-way through the mountains. The tiny carts were the best means known to move the mountains of earth necessary to construct a bed for the steel rails tying the nation together. (SPTC)

A RAILROAD BUCKER SNOWPLOW crew pauses during the winter of 1867 near Cisco, about ninety-two miles from Sacramento. Snow drifts in the Sierra Nevada often grew to a depth of 30 feet, and it required eight wood-burning locomotives behind a single plow to push through and clear the tracks. (SPTC)

THE FIRST RAILROAD STATION IN LOS ANGELES was in operation at the corner of Alameda and Commercial streets in 1869. This particular train was one of the Los Angeles & San Pedro Railroad. (SPTC)

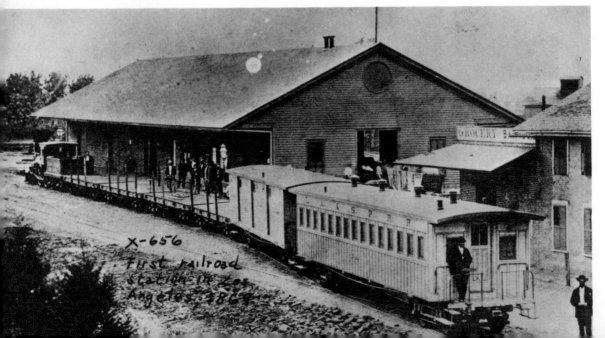

VINEYARD WORKERS load the raw material for an 1870 vintage wine from grapes harvested in one of many vineyards in the Buena Vista area. (Redwood)

CHAMPAGNE CORKING is under way at a Sonoma winery in the early 1870s. Grapes and wine came to California with the Spanish missionaries, and, until the middle of the nineteenth century, the so-called "Mission" grapes supported a growing industry in the state's mountain valleys. During the 1850s, experimentation was started with grape-vine cuttings imported from the wine districts of Europe, many of which thrived in the mild climate and the longer summer season of California, becoming the basis of an important economic factor. There were 26,500,000 grape vines by the 1870s, and more than 5,000,000 gallons of various wines produced by 139 wineries, much of it shipped to Boston and New York. The center was Los Angeles where forty-three wineries produced gross profits of $339,452. (WI)

[41]

THE CAPITAL OF CALIFORNIA was moved from one community to another until it finally settled down in Sacramento. The Capitol in Sacramento was completed in 1874, and this view, not long afterwards, shows a strong European influence in the classical building. (SPNB)

THE FIRST INDUSTRIAL HOSPITAL was built in the West in 1867 by the Central Pacific Railroad at Sacramento. Here, staff members, patients, and neighborhood children pose for a photo shortly after the hospital was completed. (SPNB)

THESE NOB HILL MANSIONS in San Francisco belonged to Mrs. Mark Hopkins and Gov. Leland Stanford. San Francisco, of all the cities in California, knew the Victorian mansions, almost all of which are gone today. (SPNB)

WAR OF 1812 VETERANS gather on San Francisco's North Main Street in front of the infamous Bella Union Hotel for an 1873 Fourth of July celebration. (LA Title)

AN EARLY STEERABLE BALLOON was exhibited at San Francisco's Woodward Garden in the early 1870s. It was one of the earliest methods of controlled flight. (LA Title)

THE FIRST SAN FRANCISCO cable-car run was a civic event on August 2, 1873. Andrew Hallidie, a local manufacturer, invented the car to deal with the hills where new millionaires were building their mansions. Hallidie's creation required the engineering of a connection to the car that would not tear it apart under a sudden jerk, and of a way for the cable to follow the contour of the street. The first run of the Clay Street Railroad Co. was made between Kearny and Jones streets on Nob Hill's Clay Street. For a time, the cable-car appeared to be the form of urban transport most cities would adopt in the future. (SFCVB)

THE SAN FRANCISCO WATERFRONT was a bustling place in 1873 with sailing ships from throughout the world berthing next to early coastal steamers. The West Coast home port of the clipper ships, San Francisco was the main conduit for trade coming into California from the rest of the world and the riches being brought out of the interior. (SPTC)

SAN BERNARDINO was the edge of wilderness when this view was taken about the time of the Civil War. It was the first California community of any size for emigrants overlanding from Salt Lake City, although it sat at the base of the San Bernardino Mountains. Holcomb Valley, a nearby gold-mining area was supplied by the valley settlement, which opened its first post office in 1852.(SPNB)

SAN GABRIEL MISSION INDIAN children play near their huts in the 1870s. (SPNB)

JUAN LARGO, better known as Long John Warner, friend of the mission Indians, poses with a group of Indians, Christmas 1875. While fine pictures of the California Indians in this period exist, it is regrettable there are no more. Interest in their plight after the closing down of the California mission chain in the 1830s and in their culture was aroused too late to capture on film many of their remarkable art forms and methods of living on an often inhospitable land. (LA Title)

SOUTHERN PACIFIC RAILROAD ENGINE NO. 34 stands on the Wilmington dock, in 1876, next to the cargo ship it is servicing. (SPTC)

THE FIRST WATER-TRANSFER implement in California may have been the Zanja water wheel. Built in San Francisco in 1782, it was shipped to Los Angeles and installed just north of Elysian Park, where it raised water thirty-six feet from the Zanja Madre (mother ditch) to flumes that went to the plaza of Los Angeles. The wheel had paddles six feet wide, each carrying a fifteen-gallon bucket. It was still in operation in 1878, when this photo was taken. (LA Title)

THE MAIN STREET OF LOOKOUT in the late 1870s: The town sprang out of the arid Argus Mountains along the pack trail that served the silver mines of Minnietta and Modoc. The almost treeless area could not furnish the charcoal required to smelt the ore, so Sen. George A. Hearst, father of the later publisher William Randolph Hearst, built beehive kilns in the Panamint Mountains' Wildrose Canyon a dozen miles away, and packed the charcoal to the mines. Lookout, and Joseph S. Birchett's store in the center of the picture, lasted until the mines paid out and then disappeared.

[48]

COMMERCIAL STREET was one of the earliest business districts of Los Angeles. In this 1870 photo business was already brisk. (LA Title)

THE UNIVERSITY OF SOUTHERN CALIFORNIA was a single $5,000 building when opened by the Southern California Conference of the Methodist Episcopal Church in 1879. Its fifty-acre campus was set in a rural environment, with Los Angeles, still a small town, three miles away. The university is the oldest private, co-educational university of any size in the West. Its first building, now known as Widney Hall, has stood on three different locations on campus and has had a wing added, but is still in use. (USC)

NEWHALL REFINERY, one of the earliest oil refineries constructed in California, was built in the late 1870s, as the inspiration of J. A. Scott, a transplanted Pennsylvania refiner, who built it to service the growing production of Pico Canyon and the Mentry properties. When it went into operation, another Pennsylvania oilman, D. G. Scofield, built a five-mile-long, two-inch pipeline to take crude oil from the wells to the refinery. It was the first pipeline in California. (SOCC)

DONA GUADALUPE SMITH'S garden in San Diego provided a quiet stopping place for Spanish-Americans during the 1870s. (SD Title)

SPANISH-AMERICAN SAN DIEGANS gather in 1874 at the Marron House in what is now called "Old Town." (SD Title)

The Land Boom: 1880 to 1890

AFTER THE 1880s in California, there was a great urge to get rich quick. California had promised that with the Gold Rush, but all the "wrong" people seemed to have been made wealthy as a result of the placer and hardrock gold lodes. So now it was land and snake oil, and often a combination of the two. If you bought one you might be buying a cliffside or a flood plain or an earthquake fissure (snake oil specials). Or you might be buying for small change what today is worth thousands, even hundreds of thousands of dollars per front foot. California still sells land to new arrivals. Alas, it still sells snake oil, too.

FORT HUMBOLDT, shown in 1885, was garrisoned by American troops from 1853 to 1865 for protection against the Indians in the district. The fort, later restored for tourists, is perched above Humboldt Bay on the southern edge of Eureka, the largest city north of Sacramento. As an army captain, Ulysses S. Grant was assigned to the post as an officer of the Fourth Infantry. It is said that the later president got his reputation for drinking while assigned to the dreary, isolated fort. (Redwood)

PIONEER PHOTOGRAPHER A. W. ERICSON stands in the door of his Arcata shop chatting with friends in the 1880s. (Redwood)

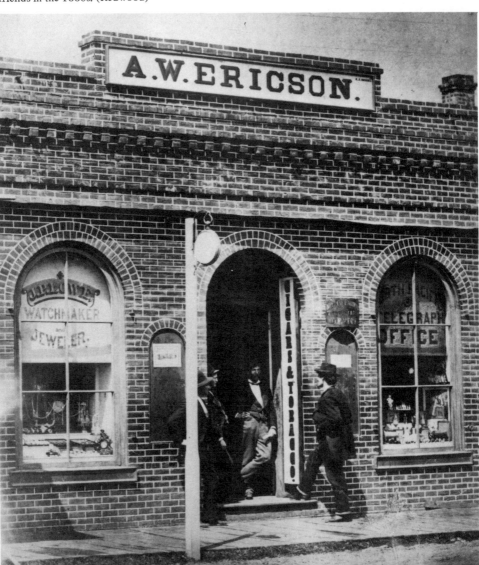

THE CARSON MANSION in Eureka was long known as the "Redwood Castle." Built in the period between 1884-1886, it is one of the nation's most photographed houses. (Redwood)

THE NORTHERN CALIFORNIA coast was dotted in the old days with "doghole ports"—anchorages dangerous and tiny for maneuvering the sailing ships that hauled lumber. The rather generous anchorage at Point Arena shows lumber schooners and a wire-chute loading device. This unusual picture was taken in 1880 by A. O. Carpenter, famous Ukiah photographer. (Redwood)

THE SECOND CLIFF HOUSE to rest on the rocky coastal escarpment at San Francisco's Point Lobos Avenue and Great Highway, was built in 1889. The first was built in 1863 as a restuarant and saloon operated by two forgotten French seamen, and flourished for about twenty years under the supervision of Capt. J. R. Foster. Adolph Sutro bought it in 1879, and operated it with little change until it was damaged when the schooner *Parallel* was driven on the rocks nearby with a cargo of 80,000 pounds of dynamite that exploded. Sutro rebuilt the house as seen here in 1896. Local residents immediately named it "Sutro's gingerbread palace." Designed this time as a plush resort, the Cliff House hosted presidents Hayes, Grant, McKinley, Roosevelt, and Taft, as well as theatre greats Sarah Bernhardt and Adelina Patti, and writers Mark Twain and Bret Harte. (Kelly)

SAN FRANCISCO'S SKYLINE in 1885 was marked by the Shot Tower on the extreme left, the shorter spire of the Masonic Temple just to the right of the tower, the massive block of the Palace Hotel, the twin turrets of the Sutter Street Synagogue, and the shorter spire of Saint Patrick Church just beyond the synagogue. (LA Title)

CENTRAL TERMINAL BUILDING on the San Francisco waterfront was built in 1877 to cover the three ferry ships operated by the Central Pacific, the Atlantic and Pacific, and the South Pacific Coast railways. As long as the ferries remained the only transportation across the bay, the terminal was the hub of streetcar, horsecar, and other traffic. It was replaced at the intersection of Embarcadero and Market Street in 1898 by the Ferry Building. (LA Title)

CALIFORNIA STREET HILL in 1885 San Francisco was a bustling business district, with horse-drawn vehicles and cable cars bringing customers to the shops that lined the cobblestone thoroughfare. (LA Title)

MARKET STREET, one of San Francisco's major thoroughfares, was a busy spot even in this 1880s photo—and count the streetcars. (SPNB)

A PARADE along Powell Street in 1885 drew throngs of San Francisco residents. (LA Title)

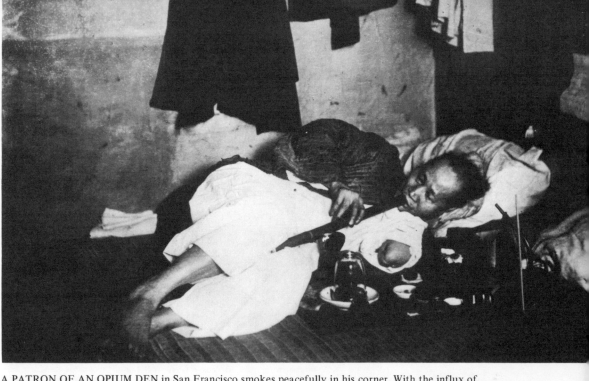

A PATRON OF AN OPIUM DEN in San Francisco smokes peacefully in his corner. With the influx of Chinese workers following the construction of the Central Pacific Railroad, opium smoking dens developed into a problem for the city. (LA Title)

GENTLEMAN HIGHWAYMAN BLACK BART single-handedly held up twenty-eight stagecoaches in the years from 1875 to 1883. Dressed in a natty linen duster and mask, Black Bart committed his robberies on foot. He became famous for his polite behavior and his taunting verses left in mail and express boxes he had looted. His real identity as a respectable San Francisco mining engineer, Charles C. Bolton, was exposed after detectives traced him through the laundry mark on a hankerchief he dropped during a robbery. He spent twelve years in San Quentin prison. (Wells Fargo)

A BOARDINGHOUSE HOLIDAY MEAL could still be a pleasant occasion despite the rugged life in the small towns of California in the latter half of the nineteenth century. This 1880 boardinghouse dining room in Bodie is set with the best china and silver and strung with foliage for a celebration.

FRANCIS MARION "BORAX" SMITH came west from Wisconsin in 1867 at the age of twenty-one, with $200 in his pockets. After working in a San Francisco borax plant, and wandering from one mining camp to another throughout the mountains, he bought a small wooded ranch in the desert. While working there, he discovered a nearby marsh that was rich with borax. From his beginnings with the Teels Marsh, Smith built Pacific Coast Borax Co. into a multi-million-dollar mining organization, retiring as president in 1913 with holdings in the firm worth $4 million. (Borax)

THE GRANDEST GRAVE ever placed in the Bodie cemetery was erected by Eli Johl, left, for his wife Lottie. Johl was a socially well-placed butcher in the city, but not important enough for the women there to accept Lottie, a former prostitute. Johl's bitterness at the town grew when Lottie died, the victim of a pharmacist's mistake, and the city fathers enforced restrictions against her. Like the Chinese in the area, they would not permit her to be buried in the church cemetery. After a bitter battle, Lottie was allowed in, but restricted to the farthest corner. Johl erected a wrought-iron fence around her grave and quickly made it into a spot that made the rest of the cemetery appear unkept.

GEN. JOHN C. FREMONT, with his wife and daughter, stands before the large tree near Santa Cruz inside which the army officer made his headquarters during the 1846 Bear Flag Rebellion and Mexican War. Fremont later became a United States senator from California. (SPNB)

WHALERS CUT UP THEIR CATCH before the whaling station at Monterey in this 1891 photo. The station was built in 1865 for Portuguese whalers to pursue the California grey whale that migrates along the coast from the Arctic to the Gulf of California.

[59]

THE FIRST DRUGSTORE in Pacific Grove was opened for business under the proprietorship of Charles Kirkam Tuttle in 1885. Steel specatacles, Diamond Dyes, and Paines Celery Compound were featured items.

AN ARMY OF SNOW SHOVELERS attacks drifts on the Central Pacific tracks in the winter of 1889-1890, when the railroad employed more than 4,000 shovelers to keep the mountain tracks clear. Supporting them in their high-altitude camps required another five hundred men to sledge in supplies and feed the workers. At Shady Run, east of Dutch Flat, ten large ranges were required to cook the meals. (SPTC)

THE FIRST TRAIN INTO SANTA BARBARA (a Southern Pacific) arrived August 19, 1887. Records from the Spanish navigator Cabrillo's exploration of the California coast in 1542, state that a large Indian village ruled by an old woman once stood near today's Santa Barbara. The area was not settled until 1782, when Fr. Junipero Serra and Governor Neve with fifty men established a presidio in response to reports that the Russians were interested in colonizing there. In the early nineteenth century, trade developed between the residents and Yankee traders, and Americans came to settle before the Mexican War turned the land over to the U. S. It almost joined the Union before the rest of the state when Commodore Stockton landed in August, 1846, ran up the flag, and left a small garrison; but a few weeks later, was attacked and given a choice between surrender and flight, the garrison fled. The town alternately prospered and starved under American rule, and experienced an abortive land boom in the 1870s. The railroad, however, started the city's development toward a wealthy residential community. (SPTC)

[61]

HORSEBACK RIDING ON THE BEACH was considered a highly fashionable way of passing time in the Santa Barbara of the 1880s and 1890s. (SPNB)

THE CITY OF VENTURA was a quiet coastal town in 1885. The prominent structure on the left side of the photograph is the old Franciscan Mission. (SPNB)

RANCH HANDS harness their teams and begin the work day in this 1880s picture of the Patterson Ranch in Ventura County. (LA Title)

EARLY ANGELENOS GATHER at the Jose Mascarel ranch, where Hollywood now stands. A husky French sea captain, Mascarel settled in Los Angeles in 1844 and married a local Indian woman. He was an important land owner in the downtown area, and became mayor of the city in 1865. (LA Title)

SAINT VIBIANA CATHEDRAL, completed in 1876, was the first Catholic cathedral built in Los Angeles. In 1936, it would become the seat of the Archdiocese of the Province of Southern California. The church sits near the corner of Main Street and Second. This 1880 picture shows the restrained Doric portico. The church, dedicated to Saint Vibiana, the child saint, has a relic of the child, taken from the catacombs of Rome, that is contained in a wax statue in a gilt sarcophagus niched above the high altar. (LA Title)

[63]

CHINESE CALIFORNIANS parade their traditional dragon during an 1880s Chinese New Year's celebration. (LA Title)

CHINESE CHILDREN pause in Old Mission Square of Los Angeles' Chinatown to eye the photographer suspiciously. As late as the 1880s the children still wear traditional Chinese dress. (SPNB)

LOS ANGELES was a sleepy little village of 14,000 people in 1883: Ever since Spanish colonization, the Indian village on the exposed Pacific shore had been out of the main stream of development. After the Mexican War, as mainly an outlet for hides, tallow, and other products from the surrounding ranchos, it had been left out of the swift growth the gold rush brought to San Francisco and the other cities closer to the mines. At this point Los Angeles, with 14,000, had fewer people than Sacramento and Oakland and much less than the 250,000 of San Francisco. It was a tough little town with a reputation for soaking up all the undesirables run out of the gold camps or the Barbary Coast. (UOC)

[65]

THE FIRST STREET LIGHT IN LOS ANgeles being installed in 1882: It was seventy feet high. (LADWP)

PERSHING SQUARE, Los Angeles, in 1885 was a peaceful park just before the land boom that would bring in throngs of people seeking their fortune. The boom was brought about by a combination of competition between railroads that cut fares from the East to $1, local efforts to promote immigration, and land promoters who saw a quick profit in subdividing unused land. Many of today's cities in the Los Angeles Basin and surrounding valleys date from the boom. Burbank, parts of Riverside, and many other cities were plotted in a frenzy of buying and selling, only to be abandoned for the most part within a few years. Others, like these two, stayed through the following lean years to make a permanent place for themselves. (LA Title)

[66]

CABLE CARS came to Los Angeles in 1885. At its inception, Henry Clay Witmer's brainstorm had tracks from the corner of Second and Spring streets along Bryson Block, Second Street, over Bunker Hill and along Lakeshore Avenue, and First Street to Belmont Avenue. The line was soon extended to intersect with a steam line in a watermelon patch that would later become Hollywood. By 1887, the Los Angeles Cable Railway Co. was organized and building lines to Boyle Heights and Downey Avenue. The viaduct across the Southern Pacific tracks, one of the landmarks of the line, shown here, was on its East Los Angeles section between San Fernando and Downey. (LA Title)

SWITCH ENGINE No.20 works in the Southern Pacific railroad yards in Los Angeles around 1885. (LA Title)

E. J. "LUCKY" BALDWIN, born in Ohio, at age sixteen had already gained a reputation there as a shrewd horse trader. At eighteen he married, and by twenty owned a general store and three boats plying between Chicago and St. Louis. Arriving in California in 1853 at the ripe old age of twenty-five, he amassed within twenty years an $8 million fortune in mining investments, from which he took the nickname Lucky. In 1875, he bought the 8,000-acre Rancho Santa Amita for $200,000 and invested another $100,000 in thoroughbred horses. He finally held 50,000 acres, including the present sites of Sierra Madre, Arcadia, and Monrovia. He planted peach, pear, apricot, loquat, palm, eucalyptus, oak, walnut, almond, persimmon, olive, camphor, and pepper trees, and experimented with growing coffee, tea, and wine grapes until the ranch was worth approximately $10 million. Married four or five times and the defendent in several law suits, Baldwin was notorious for his affairs with women. He died on his ranch in relative poverty at the age of eighty-one. Part of the ranch became the Los Angeles State and County Arboretum.

LOS ANGELES BICYCLE CLUB MEMBERS, with their high-wheel bikes, pause in front of the Agriculture Park roadhouse in 1887. (LA Title)

THE LUGO HOUSE was one of the first two-story adobe structures built in Los Angeles. Don Vicente Lugo built his home in 1840. By 1865, it was the home of St. Vincent's College, the parent school of Loyola University and the first college in Southern California. In this 1886 picture, the house has become occupied by a Chinese restaurant and a shoemaker's shop. (LA Title)

SANTA MONICA'S ARCADIA HOTEL was one of the fashionable resort hotels along the Pacific Coast from the time of its 1887 opening. It was named in honor of Arcadia Bandini Baker, wife of Col. Robert Baker, one of the city's founding fathers. In addition to other comforts, the hotel offered its guests rail-mounted tram cars for getting around.

REDONDO BEACH was one of the upcoming tourist cities in the nation in 1889 with the Hotel Redondo and its attendant tent city about to open. Relatively cheap and easy rail transporation from Los Angeles and other areas of Southern California brought visitors to the Carnation Gardens, with some twelve acres of carnations constantly in bloom, and the so-called gemstone beach, the only one of its kind in the world, where in much of the northern portion mounds of pebbles five to six feet deep and forty to fifty feet wide lay on the sand. Here could be found moonstones, moss and flower stones, a stone that looked much like a ruby, and other semiprecious jewels. Once this was known, the beach teemed with visitors. A major controversy grew about people taking the stones away, but before anything resulted, construction firms raided the beach and used the stone in their buildings. (CRB)

THIS MASSIVE HOTEL was constructed in South Pasadena between 1884 and 1886 only to burn down before it could be occupied or even named. (SPNB)

THE PROGRESS OF SOUTH PASADENA is evident in this photo of the Santa Fe Railroad station in 1886. The railroad came to the city, eliminating the stagecoach line from Los Angeles, in 1885. Despite the newness of the project, construction materials can be seen piled in the background. (LA Title)

AN INDIAN RANCHERIA in the desert country of Southern California: Back-country photographs of this period, 1886, are extremely rare. This one does tell the dress, housing, and transportation that was adopted by the Indians probably not involved in the mission experiment. (SD Title)

WALONG OR TEHACHAPI LOOP was one of the many engineering feats required by the California mountains. Here the trains had to come out of a tunnel and make a complete circle to deal with the odd grades in the area. (SPTC)

THE STAR NO. 1 OIL WELL, an early producer in the oil-rich Pico Canyon field, was drilled in 1884 and yielded seventy-five barrels a day from 1,650 feet. First commercial use of California was in 1885 when Gen. Andreas Pico, brother of the state's last Mexican governor, gathered seepage from pits in a canyon near Newhall and sold it as a medicine, a lubricant, and as lamp fuel. Earlier, Indians and Mexican settlers had collected tar from oil seeps to seal the seams of their roofs and boats. Later, some miners began to drive shafts into oil sands near the surface and collect the seepages. Difficulties with the stratified rock, vast differences between California and Pennsylvania oil, and the distance from Eastern markets slowed the industry's development. By 1886, California had produced 1,436,000 barrels, but before it became one of the top three production states in the U. S., a lot of companies merged or went bankrupt. (UOC)

[72]

THREE FORMS OF TRANSPORTATION are depicted in this 1886 photograph of the San Diego waterfront adjacent to the Russ Lumber Co., at the foot of Fourth Street. (SD Title)

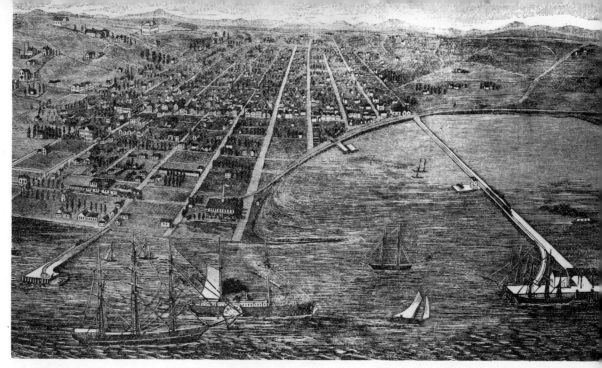

SAN DIEGO BAY AND CITY as seen by an artist in 1883. (SD Title)

SAN DIEGO'S FOURTH STREET was still a dirt road in 1887 but it already had a streetcar. (SD Title)

THE DEL MAR HOTEL stood alone in 1887 in a sparcely settled landscape near what was a popular health spa until the crash of 1888. Jacob S. Taylor, a Texas oilman, had built the hotel to take advantage of the popularity of the area and the expected growth of the subdivision around it, but all was left vacant the following year. The hotel burned in 1890. (SD Title)

SAN DIEGO'S OLD TOWN DISTRICT was a frequent gathering spot for Spanish-American residents during the 1880s. (SD Title)

THE END OF THE LAND BOOM came to San Diego in 1888. "For Sale" signs became one of the dominant features of the city's scenery. One day the Hotel Del Coronado had been opened with a special train of sightseers from Chicago, the number of business and professional men in the city had tripled to 975, property values had also tripled to $13,182,171, and land speculators were predicting a population of 150,000 for the city. The next day, more than $2,000,000 had been withdrawn from banks, and people were fleeing the area. Many of the planned cities quickly disappeared, hotels built in the middle of what were to be subdivisions stood alone, and all of the steam transportation systems but three short lines went out of business. According to the federal census of 1890, San Diego had a population of 16,159, a loss of more than half its population. (SD Title)

The Period of Expansion:
1890 to 1900

CALIFORNIA'S initial flurry of growth was based on the Gold Rush. But it was the Gold Rush merchants, not the miners, who became rich. To nurture the new California merchants, there had to be transport, buildings, fraternal societies, schools, agriculture, and entertainment.

California residents, some recent transplants from the more elegant East, some already second and third generation West Coast folks, enjoyed a measure of finery in their dress, ornamentation in their buildings, and good food and drink at their tables. It was a mix of sophistication and the primitive. The basic, fundamental pull of the frontier had brought people to California who were changed because of the new geography, but who still clung to some of the old values. The effect was dynamic, healthy, vigorous, and to a degree, puzzling. After all, the new Golden State was now only a half century old—a mere youngster. Yet its vitality was reckoned with around the world.

LADIES RISK THEIR WHITE DRESSES on Ukiah's State Street to march in the town's Fourth of July parade in the 1890s. (Redwood)

THE PACIFIC COAST LAWN TENNIS CHAMPIONSHIP of 1892 was played at the Hotel Rafael in San Rafael on July 4. The hotel burned in the 1930s. (Redwood)

REDWOOD LOGGERS assemble on a massive stump for their picture sometime in the 1890s. To their right is a Dolbeer side-spool donkey engine that replaced oxen for dragging logs out of the forest. (Redwood)

A LUMBER TRAIN pulls out of the Millwood area of the Sierra Nevada. Beginning in force in the 1890s, millions of board feet of redwood trees were slashed out of the California mountains before federal and state governments started reserving some of the timber in national parks and forests.

SEVEN SPAN OF OXEN drag redwood logs over a "skid road" in the Humboldt redwood groves in the 1890s. The roads were constructed over the soft, loose earth by laying logs side by side and filling the gaps between them with dirt. (Redwood)

REDWOOD CROSS SECTION, fifteen feet in diameter, is measured by the Pacific Lumber Co.'s logging superintendent, Dan Newell, before the log is shipped to the 1893 Chicago World's Fair. (Redwood)

THE COAST GUARD ICEBREAKER *Bear* operated along the California coast from 1885 to 1929. The 198½-foot barkentine was the first Coast Guard vessel to serve as an ice breaker. Her first assignment was in the Pribilof Islands off Alaska in search of the crew of the lost bark *Amethyst*. Here, the *Bear* is anchored in pack ice as she works her way along the northern Alaska coast to free the trapped Coast Guard cutter *Corwin,* about 1890. In addition to freeing ships from the ice, the *Bear* brought federal law to the Alaska coast. She always carried sufficient food to save native villages from starvation. (USCG)

HISTORY'S MOST FRUSTRATED TRAIN ROBBERS, Jack Brady and Sam Browning, used bicycles for transportation and attempted four robberies in the Sacramento area in the mid-1890s. In their first robbery, they took only $5.00 from a track walker because the $5,000 from the train they robbed was stolen by a tramp who saw them bury it. In their next try, the engineer fixed the engine so they could not move it when they tried to use it for their getaway. In another, gunfire scared them off. In the fourth, they argued among themselves, forgot to bring the dynamite for the safe, and decided to settle for robbing the passengers. Browning was killed by a sheriff on the train. Brady killed the sheriff, and was later captured and sentenced to life in Folsom prison.

Above: OAKLAND'S IDONA PARK was a favorite spot for ladies and children to stroll during the 1890s. (LA Title)

Facing page, top: ELECTRIC LINES already laced Oakland's Washington Street as early as this 1890 photo (LA Title)

Right: STOCKTON'S CHANNEL: This 1890 view taken from the courthouse, shows the boardinghouses in the left foreground and the flouring mills behind. Stockton was historically an important city, even though it was deep in the interior of the state. (LA Title)

TRADITIONAL DRESS in San Francisco's Chinatown, largest in the West, prevailed long after this group scene was taken in the 1890s. (SPNB)

CHINESE DOCTORS' PATIENTS in early California stepped into a different world when they entered an outer office that could be in Peking. (LA Title)

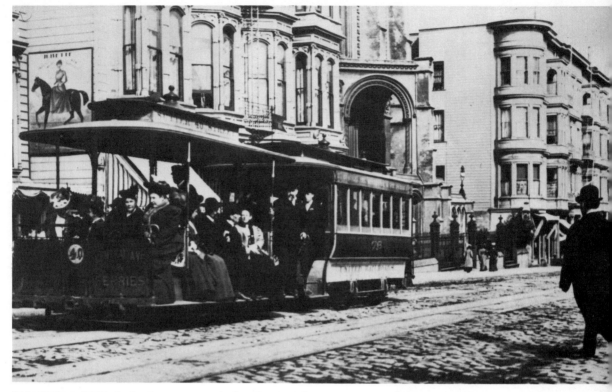

STREETCAR CITY, that's what many people thought of old San Francisco. In addition to the colorful cable car, which still remains in the hilly community, San Francisco has enjoyed numerous other streetcar varieties.

SAN FRANCISCO'S WATERFRONT still teemed with sailing ships in the last two decades of the nineteenth century, despite the influx of steamships. The ships and the horse-drawn vehicles are suggestions of the rough and ready past, but the steam boilers sitting on the dock indicate the direction the future will take.

THE GUNS OF FORT POINT glare forbiddingly across the entrance to San Francisco Bay. Built by American troops near the former site of Spanish Castillo de San Joaquin in 1853, it was designed to house 600 soldiers and 126 cannon. These eight-inch Columbaids, able to fire a 65-pound cannon ball two miles, were in place until about 1900 although the fort was abandoned in 1886, when more powerful artillery made brick forts obsolete. The fort was used as a base of operation for construction of the Golden Gate Bridge, and during World War II, it was equipped with searchlights and rapid fire cannon to protect submarine nets across San Francisco Bay. It was declared a national historic site in 1970. (NPS)

BRIG. GEN. HARRISON G. OTIS of the California Volunteers (in the dark blouse) stands in December 1898 with Maj. Gen. Arthur McArthur, members of Gen. McArthur's staff, and officers of the First Battalion, 20th Kansas Regiment (in the white uniforms) in Manila, during the Spanish-American War. Otis, publisher of the Los Angeles *Times* for thirty-one years, was appointed to his rank at the beginning of the war when the Seventh Regiment of the California State Militia was raised. He served in Manila, but fears that the Southern California coast might be raided kept the regiment in camp at the Presidio of San Francisco throughout the war. At the time of this photograph, General McArthur was commander of the North Line in the Philippines. He later became the first military governor of the islands under American rule. (Times)

SPANISH-AMERICAN WAR VOLUNTEERS from California are greeted by crowds along the streets and balconies when they arrived in San Francisco. These men were members of the G Company, Fifth Regiment. (LA Title)

PARASOLS AND DERBY HATS dominated the gathering at U. S. Senator Leland Stanford's Palo Alto farm on October 1, 1891, for the dedication of Stanford University. The senator and Mrs. Stanford, formerly Jane Eliza Lathrop, gave the land and endowed the university in memory of their son, Leland Stanford, Jr., who died from typhoid during an 1884 European tour. The bearded senator, standing, installed David Starr Jordan as the university's first president. Later President of the United States Herbert Hoover was a member of the first graduating class. (Stanford)

SERIOUS STUDY was the hallmark of Stanford University students in 1895. Despite their formal dress and studious looks, however, their dormitory room is decorated much like that of later-day students. (Stanford)

A CAMP ON IRON FORK of the San Gabriel River is occupied by, left to right, George Trogden; E. V. Lucas; Pearl Trogden, the elder Trogden's daughter; Ralph Fallows. The tent in this 1898 photo is constructed by throwing a canvas over wooden-slab walls.

GRAPES ARE UNLOADED in the 1890s at Alameda County's Warm Springs Vineyard and winery, which belonged to Josiah Stanford, brother of former governor and senator, Leland Stanford, a founder of the Central Pacific Railroad. Before the turn of the century, many of the state's wealthier men found important profits in the wine industry. Stanford's wines were a featured attraction at the famous Hotel Del Monte. (WI)

NATURALIST JOHN MUIR sits on a log in Yosemite National Park in the 1890s. The Scottish-born scientist abandoning "mechanical inventions" for "the inventions of God," spent much of the rest of his life, trekking through the wilderness and writing of its glory. His writings are credited as instrumental in establishing the U. S. Forest Service, Yosemite National Park, Sequoia National Park, Mount Rainier National Park, Petrified Forest National Park, and parts of Grand Canyon National Monument. He was the first scientist to show that glacier ice cut the valleys of the Sierra Nevada, and one of the designers of the 1891 law authorizing forest reserves. Muir presented his views to Theodore Roosevelt during the president's visit to Yosemite. In the rest of Roosevelt's administration, 148 million acres were added to the national forests, twenty-three national monuments were established, and five national parks were created. (NPS)

JOHN MUIR'S HOME from 1890 until his death in 1914 was declared a national historic site in 1964. The house has been restored to the form it had when he resided there, and more than eight acres of what was once a 2,600-acre ranch is being made into a miniature of the orchards and vineyards that once grew in this suburban area. (NPS)

BRIDAL VEIL FALLS at Yosemite National Park breaks through the escarpment and plummets into the valley in a flurry of white spray. The waterfall is one of the dominant features of Yosemite Valley, the heart of the 1,200-square-mile park in California's Sierra Nevada mountain range. (UPRR)

MONTEREY'S MAIN STREET undergoes repairs by a man with a shovel in the 1890s.

WINFRED TUTTLE was the first telephone operator in Pacific Grove.

A LADY'S TRAIL GEAR was rough, ready, and functional. Here, Ada Delvey travels the coast trail in the areas around Pacific Grove, her horse, dog, and rifle her only companions. (Myers)

SULKY-BORNE SCHOOL CHILDREN Millcent Daily and Andrew Myers prepare for a day of classes in the Pacific Grove area. (Myers)

CARSON AND COLORADO RAILROAD crewmen stop to chat with teamsters building the first highway over Montgomery Pass. The railroad, nicknamed the "Slim Princess," ran from Mound House, outside Carson City, Nevada, to a spot north of Bishop, California, and ended at Keeler, near Owens Lake. The portion of the line between Laws and Keeler was still in operation into the 1950s (Stevens)

COURT HOUSE PARK AND MARIPOSA STREET provided a break in the buildings of downtown Fresno during the 1890s. (LA Title)

"OLD DINAH," a Best steam tractor, was purchased in 1894 to replace the twenty-mule teams that hauled borax ore to the railroad. Francis Marion "Borax" Smith, president of Pacific Coast Borax Co., bought the 15.5-ton tractor because he did not like the slowness of the mule teams. The tractor would travel up to four miles an hour on rear wheels eight feet in diameter, with steel tires from two to five feet wide and three-quarters of an inch thick, and a front tire five feet in diameter. Her boiler consumed 2,500 pounds of fuel for the twelve-hour round trip from Borate to Daggett. Old Dinah is now on display at Death Valley's Furnace Creek Ranch. (Borax)

JOHN RYAN was an engineer for "Borax" Smith during construction of the Tonopah & Tidewater Railroad. Smith had planned the line to connect with the San Pedro, Los Angeles & Salt Lake Railroad. But when work started, Montana's Sen. William A. Clark, owner of the connecting line, started sabotage to halt construction. When the road was completed despite his efforts, Clark refused to permit connection to his line. With the ore deposits in the Borate mine running out, Ryan packed equipment and work gangs overland for one hundred miles (from Las Vegas to Ludlow) and connected Smith's line with the Santa Fe, extended it to the Lila C borax mines and later on to Gold Center, Goldfield, and Tonopah. Ryan later became general manager of the Lila C mines at Ryan Camp, named in his honor. (Borax)

JOHN W. S. PERRY was Pacific Coast Borax's superintendent of the Harmony Borax Works when he added a page to American history by designing the borax wagons the famous twenty-mule teams would pull in and out of Death Valley and the California desert. After ordering construction on the first ten, he laid out the route the teams would follow from Harmony to Mojave. He later became superintendent of Pacific Coast Borax Co. (Borax)

RANDSBURG in the El Paso Mountains was a thriving mining camp at the time of this 1897 picture. Gold was first discovered on the slopes of Rand Mountain in 1893. Mining camps soon sprang up, and the entire district, mountain, and one town were named after the fabulous gold-mining district of South Africa. The richest mine in the area, the Yellow Aster, had yielded $10 million in gold by 1925, and enough tungsten ore mined with the gold to pay all the expenses, making the gold ore clear profit. The Yellow Aster was a "glory hole" mine— an open pit operation. (LA Title)

[94]

BONES FROM ANCIENT BURIAL GROUNDS uncovered by the wind in the Channel Islands: On Santa Rosa Island in the 1890s, two pot-hunters pose with an assortment of Indian relics—pestles, whole and broken stone mortars, skulls, and other bones. Two of the islands now are part of the National Park Service, two are operated by the military, one is a tourist resort (Catalina), and the others are privately owned. Fossil bones of a prehistoric dwarf mammoth have also been found on one of the islands.

THE FIRST TWO POLICEWOMEN in Los Angeles. Their names have become obscure over the years, but they were obviously proud of their new badges. (LA Title)

OFFICE BUILDINGS ON MAIN STREET in Los Angeles were ornately decorated and flag-pole bedecked in 1890, but the street was still dirt. From the sign on the building, lamp mantels were an important item of commerce, and stables were located as conveniently as our parking garages are today. (LA Title)

LOS ANGELES WAS AN OIL BOOM TOWN in 1895. Two years earlier, Edward L. Doheny dug a wildcat well with a pick and shovel on a city lot just west of downtown. It started producing forty-five barrels a day, and the rush was on. Within five years, 200 oil companies were organized, 2,500 wells were sunk, and houses were destroyed to make way for oil rigs, built so close together they resembled the "holes in a pepperbox." When the city council banned oil wells as a public nuisance, many residents discovered they needed a new water well. The council could not ban drilling for water, and if this just happened to produce oil, the drillers could not be held responsible. The local oil soon cut the price of a barrel of crude oil to twenty-five cents. This oil was the second boom Los Angeles experienced between 1885 and 1895. Developing national awareness of the Southern California climate, the opening of competing Southern Pacific and Santa Fe rail service which resulted in a fare-cutting war, and rampant land-development speculation had started the first. By the time the fictions were recognized and the boom turned into a bust in 1887, the population had jumped to 50,000. (Union)

OIL-WELL CREWS of the late nineteenth century were a hard-bitten lot of dreamers. Some were miners who had given up on the promised riches of the gold and silver camps; others were experienced hands from the Pennsylvania oil fields. The crew of Robertson Well No.1, who posed for this picture in 1890 with their youthful visitors, included (standing from left to right) Ed Scholl and two children, John Millard, Ben Robertson, Ed Elkins, and another unidentified visitor. Seated from left to right were E. E. Chamberlain, Charley Millard, an unidentified man, Robert Cruson and his son Tom. (Union)

AGRICULTURAL PARK in the heart of Los Angeles, seen here around 1900, was established by the Southern District Agricultural Society as a fairgrounds and race course. When their efforts failed in 1892, the site was unused until Exposition Park opened on 114 acres of it in 1910, operated jointly by the state, county, and city. (LA Title)

138B
HILARIO IBARRA AND HIS FAMILY pose for an 1890 family portrait next to their Los Angeles home's cactus hedge. (LA Title)

HORSE CARS, such as this one whose route ran through the University of Southern California campus, were an important mode of transportation in Los Angeles during the last decade of the nineteenth century and the first decade of the twentieth. The austere wooden benches were softened somewhat by the spring-mounted wheels, while drapes, seen tied back here, gave passengers some protection from the elements. (USC)

THE HORSECAR BARN of the Los Angeles & Vernon Street Railway, at Twenty-second and Central Avenue, was an important hub of the Los Angeles transportation system in 1890 (Pierce)

A CHINESE STORE in Los Angeles is decorated for friends visiting during the 1890 Chinese New Year. (LA Title)

PETE "NIGGER" JOHNSON was a sometime preacher and politician in Los Angeles' Chinatown of the 1880s and 1890s. (LA Title)

THE FIRST "BOOM" HOTEL IN GLENDALE, shown in 1890, was yet to be occupied by guests when the bottom dropped out of the land market. Until 1924, the building was used by the Glendale Sanitarium, and later by the St. Hilda School for Girls. (LA Title)

SAN BERNARDINO'S E Street depicted a slower, more placid lifestyle in this 1895 photo. (LA Title)

A COAHUILLA INDIAN WOMAN near the Palm Springs area grinds meal in 1897, using traditional mano and metate. (LA Title)

CITRUS PICKERS pause for a picture near Fullerton in the 1890s: Lemons and oranges were brought to the valleys of California by the early Spanish missionaries. By the last decade of the nineteenth century, the seedless navel orange was introduced, and many growers were finding a ready market for their golden trove. (Sunkist)

CHINESE CITRUS WORKERS wash lemons on a farm near Arlington around 1890. Throughout the second half of the century, citrus "gold" was second only to gold dug from the mountains or from streams. Ambitious growers sold all they could grow to the mountain mining camps, or to the East on the new railroads. a full carload of oranges survived a month-long trip to St. Louis and became the marvel of the residents. Supervising this group is farm-owner E. A. Little, a citrus pioneer in the River-side area. (Sunkist)

[102]

FRUIT PACKERS grade and pack citrus in a Covina Citrus Association shed just before the turn of the century. (Sunkist)

THE SOUTHERN CALIFORNIA CITRUS FAIR gets underway in a hall bedecked with fruit in 1895. In those days, when the California fruit industry was suffering from over-production, citrus fairs suddenly became the rage, celebrating practically anything. Pasadena's 1885 fair was more a demonstration of civic pride than an industry show. A Colton fair made more ado about the resident lawmen, the Earp brothers, than citrus fruit. They did, however, engender a high degree of enthusiasm, and were the ancestors of the annual National Orange Show at San Bernardino. (Sunkist)

THE MAIN DRAG of Anaheim in Orange County would later earn fame as part of a Jack Benny radio "Anaheim, Azusa, and Cucamonga" routine; and as the site for Disneyland. But in 1890, when this photo was taken, a trolley car approaches down a dirt street lined with horse-and-buggy folks. (SPNB)

BAYONETS FIXED, the Santa Ana Women's Marching Club poses in full-battle regalia in the 1890s on French Street where, later, the lady militants moved over to make way for the Santa Ana Ebell Club. (SPNB)

THE HOTEL REDONDO, the pride and one of the main tourist attractions of the Redondo Beach community in 1890, stood in palacial splendor on a hill just above the beach. The hotel, a sister to the still-standing Hotel Del Coronado on Coronado Island, had 225 rooms, baths on every floor, and special wallpaper for men in some rooms and for women in others. It had a tennis court, an 18-hole golf course, and music in the dining room nightly. The hotel's grand ballroom was frequently the scene of lavish events, and the hotel auditorium occassionally featured grand opera. The hotel was surrounded by sumptuous grounds, palm trees, flower beds, shrubs, and of course, always the beach. It was sold and torn down around 1925 for its lumber. (CRB)

THE HOTEL REDONDO'S broad lawns made a comfortable couch for young men taking a seaside holiday. (CRB)

OLD SAN GABRIEL was founded after the establishment of Mission San Gabriel in 1771. It was from this mission that Spanish governor Felipe de Neve set out in 1781 with forty-four soldiers, Indians, and colonists to found the pueblo of Los Angeles. This picture is San Gabriel as it was in 1890.

JAPANESE WORKERS build the Mount Wilson Toll Road shortly before the turn of the century. The mountain was named for Benjamin Davis Wilson who blazed a trail to its summit in 1864, ostensibly as the first white man to reach the top. When he arrived, however, he found two abandoned cabins, which it was thought belonged to bandits who had raided the missions San Gabriel and San Luis Obispo and stole 3,000 head of horses before the advent of American rule. The 5,710-foot peak in the San Gabriel range near Pasadena was a popular hiking area. In 1904, the first telescope of what was to become the Mount Wilson Observatory was installed on its top.

THE FIRST CABIN OF THE PRESTIGIOUS CREEL CLUB, near Los Angeles, was completed in 1890. Early club members in this photo of the new cabin were prominent Angelenos: U. Q. Tufts and Mary Persinger are standing, and H. W. O'Nielvery, H. L. MacNeil, William Cardwell, Fred A. Walton, Judge W. P. Wade, and James Cuzner are sitting on the roof.

PROF. THADDEUS S. C. LOWE and a party of friends out for a day in Lowe's tally-ho: Lowe, well known for his exploits as a balloonist for the Union side of the Civil War, started a gas production business in Los Angeles in the late 1880s. He was later instrumental in construction of the railroad up Mount Lowe, named in his honor. The professor, also an inventor who contributed to the creation of the electric refrigerator, eventually became a millionaire.

BEAN THRASHING on the Dan Freeman ranch at Centinela in the 1890s. Freeman was a Canadian who settled in the Los Angeles area in 1873. He purchased 25,000 acres of land so arid that it was considered worthless for farming or cattle, stocked it with sheep, and became one of the area's most influential residents. (LA Title)

CATALINA ISLAND BEACHES were favorite spots for Sunday outings at the time of this 1897 group picture.

THIS 4,600-FOOT-LONG-WHARF at Santa Monica was built in 1891 in the midst of a battle over
the location of port facilities for Los Angeles, which had no natural harbor. Ships were forced to anchor outside the mud flats at San Pedro and transfer their cargo ashore in lighters and surf boats.
With more traffic through San Pedro during the gold rush, and national attention focusing on California, interest in an improved harbor grew. Around 1872, a $200,000 breakwater was built at San Pedro,
but Southern Pacific Railroad president, Collis P. Huntington, uninterested in expansion here, began
working for construction of a port at Santa Monica. His firm built the long wharf, created a buoy
system, and started efforts to get the government to build a breakwater. With Sen. Stephen M. White
of Los Angeles fighting for the San Pedro location and Huntington demanding the Santa Monica location, governmental commissions conducted a series of investigations, finally settling on the "free"
port at San Pedro over the Southern-Pacific-controlled Santa Monica location. The wharf was demolished in 1921. (CRB)

SQUARE-RIGGED MERCHANTMEN still tied up at San Diego's Santa Fe wharf in 1850. (SD Title)

HARBOR FACILITIES ON SAN DIEGO BAY were already well developed in 1890. The steamer *City of Topeka* is tied up to the Pacific Steamship wharf in the left background, behind the Silver Gate Bath House and Star Boat House which extended from Fifth Street pier. The sailing vessels on the right side of the photo are tied up to the east end of the Santa Fe wharf. (SD Title)

SAN FRANCISCO FIREMEN and their equipment pay a formal visit to the San Diego County Courthouse in 1894. (LA Title)

157
THE HORTON HOUSE was the scene of many San Diego civic celebrations like the parade taking
place around the plaza in 1890. It was completed in 1870 by Alonzo Horton, the father of San Diego,
and one of the many temporary millionaires common to California then. He no sooner finished his
hotel when he lost his fortune in the economic collapse of 1870. He survived living frugally on the
money the city paid him for purchase of the plaza. His thirty-four-year-old landmark was torn down
in 1905 to make way for the U. S. Grant Hotel. (SD Title)

AMOS G. THROOP made his fortune in the Chicago business community and came to Pasadena only after retiring at seventy. He founded Throop University, later the California Institute of Technology, because he saw the standard American education as too bookish. He was eighty when he started his school in which students would learn by doing. His $200,000 fortune went to get it off to a sound start. (Cal Tech)

THE CALIFORNIA INSTITUTE OF TECHNOLOGY, one of the nation's pioneer manual-training institutions, had thirty-five students, ranging in age from seven to twenty, in its first class. The schedule included woodworking, physics, cooking, biology, clay modeling, piano, voice, painting. and drawing. By 1907, the Pasadena school, under the direction of astronomer George Ellery Hale, announced plans to become a "technical school of college rank the equal of any in the country." Hale, the first director of Mount Wilson Observatory, saw the school's manual-training role being absorbed by public schools, and the institution ready for transition. The university's trustees, Hale, Dr. Norman Bridge, Arthur H. Flemin, Henry M. Robinson, J. A. Culbertson, and C. W. Gates set out to transform the small vocational school into one of the world's centers of scientific research. (Cal Tech)

AH QUIN AND HIS FAMILY: The
name of the formal photographer of this
1899 picture of a San Diego Chinese
family is lost, but his work has left a
priceless example of one of the most
important ethnic groups that settled in
all corners of the Golden State (SD Title)

PROPRIETORS OF THE JAPANESE
Bazaar on San Diego's Fifth Street await
customers in this 1889 photograph.
(SD Title)

STUDENTS OF FATHER UBACH'S INDIAN SCHOOL at Casa De Aguirre in San Diego's Old Town pose for class photos in the 1890s. (SD Title)

FRARY & FOSTER stagecoaches linked the railroads to the gold camps of Julian and Banner in the 1890s. As the southern gold strikes developed into paying ventures—there were twenty mines in the Julian-Banner district by 1894—the railroads extended their lines from San Diego to Foster at the foot of the rapidly rising mountains. They got no further. From there, stagecoaches, like this one stopped before the Belleview Hotel in San Diego, carried passengers into the mining camps. (SD Title)

An Age of Innocence: 1900 to 1910

CALIFORNIA was always a land of "room enough" and when the tracks were laid and the roads were paved—even just a few at a time—there was time to stop and think, to ponder wars, and, to dream of the incredible things to come.

California was big and there were mountains to climb and explore. And in the mountains the explorers would find timber in prodigious quantity; they would find minerals in astonishing abundance. The desert was rich in mineral wealth. The stream-nourished valleys held good soil for growing anything. Hence the richness came as Nature's bounty, an offering from the land. And the people did unwise things in their harvest of the timber and the minerals and the farm lands, but the abundance cloaked their innocence or greed, and still the state offered more. Wise men became wealthy. Ambitious men became powerful. And the innocents worked for both and the state prospered.

WELL-KNOWN STAGECOACH
driver Clark Foss starts from Calistoga
Springs with a party of visitors to the
Geysers. Foss was immortalized in the
story "Silverado Squatters." (Redwood)

A RACK OF CROSS-CUT SAWS, freshly
sharpened, awaits loggers cutting the
huge timber in Shasta National Forest
around 1900.

THE BOOLE TREE was the only redwood in the Converse Basin that did not fall under the ax and crosscut saw. From 1897, the 1,000-foot-deep basin that Charles P. Converse had discovered in the mountains yielded up to 8,000 trees. Why this particular giant, found in 1903, was left is unknown. It was 269 feet tall, 112 feet in circumference, and 35 feet in diameter at the base, easily the largest tree. It was named in honor of the Sanger Lumber Co.'s general manager, Frank Boole.

LADIES in white floor-length dresses brave the dirt streets, dusty carriages, and streetcars along Sacramento's K Street in 1905. (LA Title)

RAPID TRANSIT: You can't do it this way now, but in 1907 you could take the Central California Traction Company streetcar from Stockton to Lodi. Stockton was and is an important port and educational center, while Lodi is known for vineyards, agriculture, and fine homes. (SPNB)

THE ST. FRANCIS HOTEL was a
San Francisco landmark, as in this
1905 photo, before it was destroyed
by the 1906 earthquake and fire.
(LA Title)

MILE ROCKS LIGHTHOUSE on the treacherous rocks a mile off Landsend in the mouth of the
Golden Gate: Constructed in 1906, the year of the San Francisco earthquake and fire, the light was
installed to avoid the sort of disaster that the S. S. *City of Rio de Janeiro* suffered five years earlier.
The ship struck the rocks there and sank with the loss of 129 lives. The seas in the area are so heavy
that the walls of the 1,500-ton foundation had to be four feet thick and steel clad. The 11,000-
candlepower light stands seventy-eight feet above the water, and can be seen eleven miles out to sea.
(USCG)

SAN FRANCISCANS flee the downtown rubble after the April 18, 1906, early morning earthquake. Numerous fires roared through the city of ninety-per-cent wooden structures, the largest proportion for any city in the U. S., bringing the death toll to 315 for the fire and earthquake. When the incident was over, 352 persons were listed missing. Approximately $500,000,000 damage was done, with 512 blocks containing 28,188 buildings destroyed. *(Below,)* Market Street burns as numerous fires started from broken gas mains and overturned oil heaters. When the city's gas works exploded, adding to the inferno, and with the total disruption of the city water system, firemen were forced to resort to dynamiting buildings in the fire's path in an effort to halt it. In the background, the San Francisco ferry building can be seen through the pall of smoke. (SPNB, Wells Fargo)

SAN FRANCISCO CITY HALL, *(above)* resembles a World War II bombed-out building in what had become known as "The Wickedest City in the World." Of all the masonry buildings in the city, the 48-second tremor did the greatest damage to the $7,000,000 city hall. Residents gather their belongings in the street *(right)* in the aftermath of the earthquake that occurred at 5:16 a.m. In the background, smoke from the fires can be seen creeping from building to building.(SPTC)

SAN FRANCISCO HOMES LEAN AGAINST EACH OTHER after the earthquake had destroyed much of the city. The well-built masonry buildings downtown were only slightly damaged, but most of the city's 400,000 residents were caught in their wooden lodging houses and homes, which were thrown into the street and against each other in a twisted mass of wreckage *(top)*. Workmen clean up the rubble. By the time the three-day fire had died out, 250,000 residents were encamped in the city parks, and another 100,000 had fled across the bay or down the peninsula. From that time until approximately mid-May, federal and state troops patrolled the city in cooperation with police and civilian committees appointed by Mayor Eugene E. Schmitz. All had orders to "shoot to kill" any looters. Despite monumental graft, $150,000,000 had been spent by 1909 in the construction of 20,000 new buildings. (SPTC, Wells Fargo)

THE BANK OF AMERICA opened first as the Bank of Italy in San Francisco on October 17, 1904, in the building on the left side of the picture. It was founded by A. P. Giannini, a commission merchant and bank director of Italian descent. The premises were destroyed during the earthquake and fire, but was the first to reopen after the disaster *(above)*. Giannini later organized the Bancitaly Corp., which became the Transamerica Corp. Through his efforts, the bank survived the attempted "raids" of Eastern interests, such as that staged in 1930 by Elisha Walker of New York, and the various financial panics that have hit the nation. He took great pride in the fact that the San Francisco Chinatown branch had none of its loans defaulted during the 1903 Great Depression. (BA)

THE COLONNADED BANK OF CALIFORNIA was the first downtown San Francisco building to rise from the rubble of the devastating 1906 earthquake and fire. Founded in 1864 in the midst of the outpouring of wealth from the Comstock Lode, its president, D. O. Mills, and the bank's owner, William C. Ralston, personally loaned Stanford, Huntington, Crocker, and Hopkins the money necessary to finance the completion of the Central Pacific Railroad. When the bank was forced to close its doors in 1875 during a battle for dominance in the Comstock, it added to the financial panic in the area, but was later reorganized to remain an important bank in the city and the West. (SFCVB)

CITY OFFICIALS, clergymen, and various dignitaries, both young and old, gathered in San Francisco's Golden Gate Park on November 17, 1907, for the unveiling of a statue of Father Junipero Serra. (LA Title)

SAN JOSE'S CITY HALL was a building of character that attracted visitors, such as the young ones in this picture in 1907. (LA Title)

179C

AN ELECTRIC LIGHT atop a high scaffold and the ornate, almost oriental domes of the post office building highlighted the view from San Jose's St. James Park in 1907. (LA Title)

YOSEMITE VALLEY, the seven-square-mile heart of Yosemite National Park in the Sierra Nevada, is a panorama of natural beauty from Inspiration Point. On the left is the breathtaking mass of stone called El Capitan. In the center of the picture is the Half Dome, and the Bridal Veil Falls spill over their cliff on the right. (USFS)

[126]

LOVER'S POINT in 1900 Pacific Grove was a popular weekend outing spot.

HOPKINS SEASIDE LABORATORY was well-known in the Monterey area at the time of this 1904 picture. The person who was described as "Doc" in the famous novel *Cannery Row,* at one time worked at the research facility.

HORTICULTURIST LUTHER BURBANK, left, and the transplanted English writer George Wharton James meet in 1905. Burbank found the rich soil and the mild climate of the Santa Rosa Valley ideal for his experiments. His efforts have produced the Burbank potato; the thornless cactus; the edible cactus; the Santa Rosa climax, the Wickson, the apple, the gold, and other varieties of the plum; the plumcot; the giant, the stoneless, and the sugar prune; Burbank cherries; Shasta daisies; giant and fragrant callas; and the Burbank, the Santa Rosa, and the peachblow rose. Wharton moved to Pasadena in 1888 and after much travel throughout the area, wrote and lectured extensively on the Spanish missions and related subjects. (Pierce)

A 1905 HUNTING PARTY at the Louie Newcomb ranch at Chilao included (left to right) Jasper Osborne, Clyde Cook, Frank Osborne, and Frank Robinson.

THE DEATH VALLEY BRASS BAND was major entertainment in 1910 at Ryan, a borax-mining desert town. Life around Death Valley ranged from difficult to impossible. With no air conditioning, the only escape from the blistering heat was by turning the few fans so they blew through wet gunny sacks. Aside from the band, about the only relaxation for the miners and their families was an occasional freezer of home-made ice cream when there was left-over ice from the Tonopah & Tidewater Railroad refrigerator cars. (Borax)

VENTURA was a growing coastal city in 1905, already feeling some of the expansion it would undergo in later periods. (LA Title)

A HORSE-DRAWN STREETCAR meets the train at Ventura on the coast about 1905. The old name for the community, taken from the mission, was San Buenaventura. (LA Title)

THE DEL VALLE FAMILY gathers for a picnic party at Camulos in 1900. Rancho Camulos in Ventura County was the home of the Del Valle family, and was the setting for part of Helen Hunt Jackson's famous novel *Ramona*, depicting the plight of the California Indian. (LA Title)

[130]

SOLDIER RESIDENTS OF THE SANTA MONICA SOLDIERS' HOME fall out for a Memorial Day review in 1905. (LA Title)

STONE RETAINING WALLS and landscaped flower beds bounded the north Broadway Street entrance to Los Angeles' Elysian Park in 1900. The ornate lamp post at the park entrance, the solitary streetcar, and the sparse houses suggest the slower tempo of life in turn-of-the-century Los Angeles.

B'NAI B'RITH SYNAGOGUE at the corner of Ninth and Hope streets in Los Angeles was an imposing building in 1902. (LA Title)

LOS ANGELES SHRINERS occupy the flower-decked carriage representing the Chamber of Commerce in the 1901 parade of La Fiesta de Los Angeles. (LA Title)

CHINESE residents of Los Angeles prepare for the Fiesta de Los Angeles parade of 1901. (LA Title)

A CHINESE NEW YEAR DRAGON prepares to march as part of the 1908 Fiesta de Los Angeles. (Pierce)

THE LABOR TEMPLE FLOAT in the 1909 Fiesta de Los Angeles parade: The spring celebration was originated in 1894, patterned after New Orleans' Mardi Gras. It rapidly grew into an important civic function. (LA Title)

DON ORMESINDO YORBA (second row, third from the left) pauses for pictures following the marriage of his daughter Naina to a member of the Arballo family in Los Angeles. Don Ormesindo's wife, a member of the Gilbert family of Baja California, stands to his right. (LA Title)

SHERIFF WILLIAM A. HAMMEL of Los Angeles and Gen. M. H. Sherman were a modern pair in 1900, driving along Hollywood Boulevard in the general's Mobile Stanhope Steamer. The general, driving the vehicle, arrived in 1889 and quickly organized the Consolidated Electric Railway Co. to provide inter-urban transportation. In coordination with Eli P. Clark, president of the Los Angeles Pacific Railroad Co., Sherman built the electric railroad to Pasadena (LA Title)

A POLICE BICYCLE SQUAD pedals along Los Angeles' Broadway Street in 1904. (LA Title)

THE BARKENTINE *FULLERTON* was one of the early oil tankers on the West Coast. Built in 1901, the ship had a capacity of 16,000 barrels. She delivered oil from California fields to Hawaii. When steamships invaded the field, the *Fullerton* was used as a barge, and was one of two towed by the steam tanker *Whittier* when it delivered to Hawaii the largest single cargo of oil to date, 34,200 barrels. The 1902 trip was the first time two barges had been towed over the 2,500-mile open-sea route by a single steamship. (UOC)

THE BURBANK THEATRE was one of Burbank's earliest theatrical houses for touring European road companies. Oliver Morosco leased the theatre in 1899, and after presenting the usual road-company fare for a while, he formed a stock company with local talent. The theatre, here depicted in 1903, sat in what had been a portion of the J. J. Warner ranch orchard. (LA Title)

CHARLES FLETCHER LUMMIS was the oracle of Los Angeles for nearly thirty years. A New England newspaperman, Lummis reached the city in 1884 after walking 3,500 miles. He spent the rest of his life writing about the California, Arizona, and New Mexico areas. Lummis founded and edited *The Land of Sunshine* magazine, served as city librarian for five years, assisted in organizing the Southwest Museum, and founded the Landmarks Club.

SANTA MONICA BOULEVARD in Hollywood was a quiet residential street in 1906. Although the dirt street already had streetcar tracks, the sign on the utility pole bars automobiles from going beyond Western Avenue. (Pierce)

CHUTES PARK at Washington and Main in Los Angeles was established on thirty-five acres in 1887 by D. V. Waldron. First called Washington Gardens, it became one of the most popular pleasure spots. Sunday afternoons saw variety shows in the small pavilion, and there was dancing for those who wished it. By 1906, the park, shown here, had added a roller coaster and water slide for the more adventurous. (LA Title)

THE "AERIAL SWALLOW" was a 1907 Burbank-based experiment in monorail transportation. The effort failed and soon became known as "Fawkes Folly." Burbank, born during the land boom of the late 1880s, languished until the coming of the Pacific Electric Railway in 1911. (LA Title)

SPINNING YUCCA FIBER was an art still known to California Indians at the time of this 1903 photo of an old man and his children. (LA Title)

THE TOLL GATE to San Antonio Canyon is opened for Mark H. Potter, F. Wheeler, Stuart Wheeler, and Mrs. F. Wheeler in 1908. The road was the automobile route up Mount Baldy east of Los Angeles. The toll for a "touring car with not over 5 persons" was seventy-five cents.

PRES. WILLIAM HOWARD TAFT surveys the Los Angeles area from the platform of his train during his 1909 visit to Southern California. (LA Title)

A RED CAR, part of Southern California's electric inter-urban train system, stops at Sierra Madre Boulevard and Baldwin in Sierra Madre in 1909. The system was basic transportation for many Southern Californians until the automobile's dominance.

TOURISTS dismount a Pacific Electric Railway Co. car to observe the orange groves around Pasadena in the early 1900s. The special cars were a major attraction used to show prospective land buyers the desirability of California real estate. (SPNB)

[140]   PRES. THEODORE ROOSEVELT plants a parent navel orange tree during ceremonies in Riverside, May 6, 1903. The seedless orange, a genetic deviant, first appeared in Brazil and later in Baja California. Two trees were brought to California, one of them to Riverside, and cuttings from them soon were in such demand that shoots sold for up to a dollar a dozen. When thieves started stripping them, the trees were surrounded with barbed wire. Here, this one was finally transplanted in front of Riverside's Mission Inn. (Sunkist)

CITRUS PACKERS at the Pomona Packing House in 1908. Cooperatives had stopped the cut-throat competition in the industry, and orange growers were undergoing a small boom in demand, started two years earlier when their California gold was introduced to the Midwest. It was the dawn of orange marmalade and all the other citrus frozen and dessert products with the advent of efficient frozen-food railroad cars. (Sunkist)

PIONEER PASADENA BALLOONIST Roy Knabenshue displays his lighter-than-air ship shortly after the turn of the century.

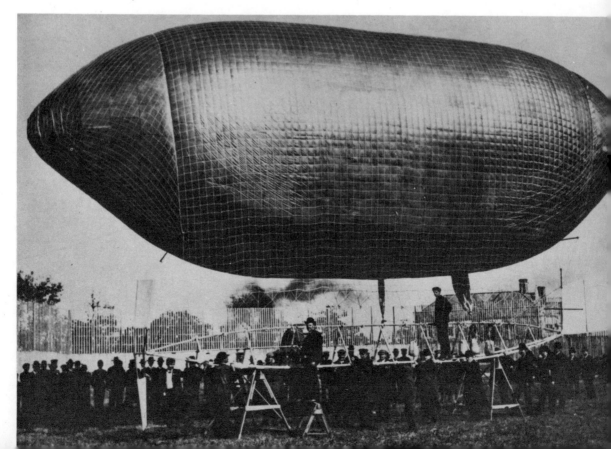

PASADENA LADIES in the 1900 Tournament of Roses: The New Year festival was started in the re-served, 1890 community to celebrate the winter blooming season, when Los Angeles and other California cities were staging festivals to attract residents and promote prestige. Originally called "Battle of the Flowers," the celebration was patterned after one in Nice, France, and in Monte Carlo. Until shortly after 1900, it included a chariot race.

THE NEW RAYMOND HILL Hotel just south of the Pasadena city limits makes a sophisticated contrast to this group on an outing around 1900. The resort quickly became popular because of its view of the surrounding town and orange groves. A wealthy residential community known locally as "gilt-edged Raymond" grew up around it. An earlier hotel there had burned in 1895.

SAN BERNARDINO, the city at the end of the Mormon Trail to California, is represented in 1903 by this new, elegant Masonic Temple. (SPNB)

BUGGY PARKING was a forerunner of things to come on San Bernardino's Third Street in 1905. (LA Title)

SPANISH-AMERICAN WAR VETERANS, calling themselves Teddy's Terrors, gather for a reunion banquet in Santa Ana in 1904. (LA Title)

Facing page: THE FOUNDATION SITE of the first telescope of the Carnegie Institution's observatory on Mount Wilson *(bottom)* was primarily planned for solar observations, but was expanded to other observations in "the necessity for seeking, among the stars and nebulae, for evidence as to the past and future stages of solar and stellar life." A total of eight telescopes eventually went into service there, including a 100-inch reflector. Specially designed trundle carts *(top)* were used to haul the first pieces of astronomical equipment to the summit. The horse was led up the steep trail, the cart rider used a wheel to guide the front wheels, and the man behind assisted in controlling and steering.

[144]

TRACK WALKERS lead a passenger train through the Colorado River flood that created the Salton
Sea, while railroaders attempt to dam the deluge. Until 1905, today's Salton Sea was only a massive
desert depression, a remnant of prehistoric Lake Cahuilla, long cut off from the Gulf of California
by the Colorado River. Early in the twentieth century, the river broke its self-created dike, poured
across the roads and railroads in the area, and filled a body of water 30 miles long, 8 to 14 miles wide,
and 83 feet at its deepest. The sea remains due to a flow from the New Alamo rivers that get drainage
from irrigation projects in the area. The sea has no outlets. (SPTC)

LA JOLLA'S Prospect Street was a sandy stretch between sparse houses in 1900. (SD Title)

THE SCHOONER *Alice McDonald* is wrecked off Point Loma Lighthouse on December 31, 1909.
The light was installed in 1854 to warn ships of the spit of land guarding the opening to San Diego
Bay. (SD Title)

The *San Diego*, a cruiser in the U.S. battle fleet as it was fitted out in 1907: A carryover from the
days of sailing ships battling side by side, most of the *San Diego's* heavy guns are along her sides. The
only hint of the future of naval armaments is in the single turrets mounted fore and aft. (USN)

THE NAVY GUNBOAT *Bennington* exploded in San Diego Bay July 21, 1905, while getting up steam for a trip to Port Harford, and 60 sailors from a total of 16 officers and 181 men were killed. Ships from throughout the bay area, doctors from all over the city, and all sorts of freight wagons and carriages hurried to help the wounded. Investigation showed that a boiler had given way, slamming into an adjacent one. Both exploded. Theaters and shops closed in mourning for the victims, who were buried in a mass grave at the cemetery of Fort Rosecrans, on a hill overlooking San Diego Bay. (SD Title)

GREAT WHITE FLEET sailors go ashore in San Diego during their trip around the world in 1908. While the fleet was in, the city hosted a nearly continuous round of parties and dinners for the officers and men of the ships, and some 50,000 visitors came to town to view the spectacle. The ships, two miles long at their anchorage, made a huge display at night with lights strung along their decks and in their riggings. (SD Title)

NEWSPAPER TYCOON E. W. Scripps, owner of the *San Diego Sun,* is shown here, booted and bearded, talking with his wife and his ranch foreman, Robert L. Clingan, in 1905. Scripps and his family settled on a ranch near Miramar and quickly became important members of the community, endowing the Scripps Institute of Oceanography, the world-famous San Diego Zoo, and many other cultural activities. (SD Title)

A DOUBLE-DECKED STREETCAR of San Diego in 1905: This car operated on Fifth and H streets and on Logan and National avenues. The weather was so pleasant that there was no protection from the elements on the upper deck. (LA Title)

THE ST. JAMES HOTEL (originally, the Santa Rosa) was one of San Diego's finest and largest during the land rush of the mid-1880s. Built by Dr. P. C. Remondono, the 160-room hotel was demolished in 1909 to make way for the Maryland Hotel. (SD Title)

NON-SAILORS found the Coronado beaches a welcome spot to relax early in the twentieth century. The pier in front of the Hotel Del Coronado is visible in the background. (SD Title)

THE TENT CITY adjacent to the Hotel
Del Coronado *(above)* was erected in
1900 by owner Adolph B. Spreckels to
attract residents of the Imperial Valley
and other desert areas to the cool shore.
When San Francisco was destroyed by
the 1906 earthquake, much of the tent
city was pulled down and sent to aid the
disaster area. A tent restaurant and
refreshment stand operated by D. C. Fox
(right) served the sun-burned
beach goers. (SD Title)

THE GREAT STORM of 1906 left
Coronado beaches a mass of pounding
waves and piled-up seaweed. Broken
pilings left from the severely damaged
Del Coronado Hotel pier can be seen
protruding at the wave line. (SD Title)

MISSION INDIAN GIRLS at the Pala School around 1900 take their mandolin lesson *(above)*, while other students relax under a shade tree with their teachers. There is a sub-mission at Pala in San Diego County, but most of the Indians living there were moved off traditional Indian lands at Warners by government edict and settled in the less-attractive site. (LA Title)

The Movies and the Airplanes: 1910 to 1920

THE LAND OF SUNSHINE inherited the motion picture industry partly because of the many days of fair weather each year. The climate was a happy one for building the new flying machines. The cities pushed back their boundaries, and people in the East, by winter, talked of California's orange groves and flowers.

Those who came to California because of the new film industry created their own folklore, which has been written about a thousand times and still has never been captured in a definitive manner. The men who came here to build airplanes gave California still another dimension. The PBY and the P-38 and the U-2 and the DC-3 all have a kind of California genesis. As it was from the beginning, California was that curious, incomparable mix. There were no yardsticks by which to measure what California was, nor where it was going. But there were millions of words to describe that whatever was happening, it was happening in California.

ISHI, THE LAST SURVIVOR of the Yahi Tribe of Stone Age people in North America, returned to Deer Creek Canyon in 1914 to show anthropologists some of the facets of his daily life. Here, he constructs a fishing harpoon *(left)*. The broken canyon lands around Mount Lassen were populated by approximately 2,000 members of the Yahi people before white men rushed into the area in response to reports of gold in the mid-nineteenth century. The tangled growth and rugged terrain of the canyon *(below),* in the foothills of volcanic Mount Lassen, provided concealment for Ishi and the last of the Yahi people for several years. Between 1852 and 1867, most of them were enslaved, were killed, or died of white-men's disease. After some white men were killed in retaliation, a program of extermination reduced the Stone Age people to twenty or thirty survivors. In 1894, there were only five, Ishi and his relatives. Ishi died in 1916, still aiding anthropologists to understand his culture. (Lowie)

PRESIDENT-ELECT HERBERT HOOVER joins conservationist Gifford Pincot, second from left, and several other men to demonstrate the massive size of the giant redwoods in the groves near Crescent City. (Redwood)

TEAMS AND WORKMEN TOIL THROUGH THE MUD to construct the northern reaches of U. S. Highway 101 (the Redwood Highway) along the Northern California coast in the period immediately before World War I. (Redwood)

AUTHOR JACK LONDON starts his trip north collecting information for the North of Bay County's Association in 1911. *Below,* London and his party have stopped in front of X. A. Philips' Store in Crescent City. The adventure writer supervised the construction of his home, Wolf House, at Glen Ellen in 1912. The house burned only one year later. (Redwood)

THE MOONY FLAT HOTEL, shown around 1915, was built near Marysville in the 1880s. One of the earliest hotels in the area, it was the temporary home of many early California families. (Myers)

POSTMEN AND ARMED MARINES convoy the military payroll from the Sacramento Post Office to Mather Air Field in 1918. The field, later Mather Air Force Base, was opened during World War I to train pilots. (MAFB)

EUGENE ELY, one of Glenn Curtiss' North Island pilots, makes the first aerial takeoff from a Navy ship as his Curtiss pusher-type plane roars off a specially improvised flight deck on the cruiser *Pennsylvania* in San Francisco Bay. The 1911 flight was the first step in convincing aging Navy admirals that the airplane had a place in future navies. (SD Title)

DRIVERS FROM THROUGHOUT STOCKTON line up in front of the city's court house for their picture to be taken in approximately 1919. (LA Title)

A PURE PIECE OF THE ORIENT was located behind the walls of this 1915 Chinese restaurant in San Francisco. A single patron occupies a lonely booth in the rear of the otherwise deserted room. (LA Title)

ACTRESS SARAH BERNHARDT, in soldier costume, appears in a February 22, 1913, complimentary performance of "A Christmas Night Under the Terror" at San Quentin Prison. (Redwood)

WILLIAM RANDOLPH HEARST, son of wealthy former California Sen. George Hearst, started his career as a newspaperman in 1887 when he took over operations of his father's conservative *San Francisco Daily Examiner* and installed some of his former classmates on the staff. He introduced the West Coast to the human-interest reporting technique developed by Joseph Pulitzer, was a prime agitator for American involvement in the Spanish-American War, and one of the inventors of the "crusading yellow sheets." Along with mining and ranching interests, William Randolph presided over a communications empire that at one time included thirty newspapers, fifteen magazines, six radio stations, and several film companies *(above, left)*. His La Cuesta Encantada—The Enchanted Hill-was probably the most fabulous private residence in the Western Hemisphere. Hearst personally supervised construction of the one-hundred-room mansion with its thirty-eight bedrooms, thirty-one baths, fourteen sitting rooms, a kitchen, movie theater, billiard room, dining hall, assembly hall, and two libraries in 1919. It sits amidst 123 acres of gardens, terraces, pools, and guest houses in the Santa Lucia Mountains, 16,000 feet above the tiny village of San Simeon. (SPNB, CDPR)

SAN FRANCISCO'S CITY HALL, constructed between 1913 and 1915, replaced the one destroyed by the earthquake and fire. The $3.5 million building was patterned after the national capitol, but to the great pleasure of Mayor James Rolph its dome was taller than the Washington version. Its rotunda was the site of Pres. Warren G. Harding's funeral, and where San Franciscans danced all night celebrating the end of World War I. (SFCNB)

BARTON'S OPERA HOUSE in Fresno, built in the 1890s, was for years one of the centers of the San Joaquin Valley for the road-show companies. A landmark and a site of pleasure for at least two generations, the Barton was torn down in 1917. *The Lure,* advertised here, dealt with white slavery, which was eyebrow raising, but it didn't keep anyone away. (SPNB)

MOUNTAINEERS PAUSE at the summit of Mount Whitney during the second decade of the century. The tallest peak in the continental United States (14,496 feet), Whitney was first conquered on August 18, 1873, by John Lucas, Charles D. Begole, and A. H. Johnson, who attempted to name the mountain Fisherman's Peak. It was finally named for Josiah Dwight Whitney, the chief of the survey.

THE HUME SAWMILL, built in the mountains north of today's Kings Canyon National Park, lies blanketed with snow in the winter of 1913. The sawmill's flume ran fifty-nine mile to Sanger, through an area of sheer granite walls, steep gorges, and thick underbrush infested with rattle snakes. It had seventeen stations along its route, thirteen with telephones. Not only was it the easiest way to get logs out of the steep country, but the loggers also built flume boats and rode them to Sanger to avoid the rough country.

SANTA BARBARA'S BAY FRONT was a fashionable, peaceful setting at the time of this 1910 picture.

MOVIE MAKERS from the American Film Co. of Santa Barbara shoot a French street scene in the midst of the West Coast city about 1915. (Ronnie)

WESTERN NOVELIST ZANE GREY works on another of his
heroic tales at his desk in his Altadena home. Even though he was a
prolific writer, fishing could always call Grey away from his work.
At left, he is shown around 1915, with the 450-pound swordfish he
caught off Catalina Island.

HORSES WERE THE DOMINANT FORM OF TRANSPORTATION on Burbank's San Fernando Boulevard as late as 1911. (SPNB)

HOLLYWOOD HOTEL was one of the central landmarks of the motion picture industry's heyday. In addition to providing the title and plot for a motion picture, the hotel in the heart of the film colony was the gathering spot for hopeful young girls who travelled to Hollywood seeking stardom. (LA Title)

"BRONCO BILLY" (Gilbert M.) Anderson was grinding out Western movies in the Edendale area of Los Angeles about 1910. The first actor-producer, Anderson set an all-time record when he made 376 films in as many weeks. He was also the first Western hero who feared and hated horses. Edendale, east of Hollywood, was home to the first flimsy movie colony in Los Angeles. It was dotted with false fronts, prop saloons, and ranch-house interiors that were constantly collapsing in the midst of a scene. (AMPAS)

THE KEYSTONE COPS and their director, Mack Sennett, made their classic Americana comedies in the Edendale area of the West Coast film industry. The cops' madcap chases and wild melees set a standard of slapstick seldom equalled. Mack Sennett, also brought Mabel Normand, Ford Sterling, Fred Mace, and Fatty Arbuckle to comedy films, along with bathing beauties and the custard pie in the face. He and other directors, always wanting as much action as they could get, sometimes kept their cameras grinding as their flimsy props collapsed, and included the debacle in the finished movie. (AMPAS)

THE BABYLONIAN ORGY SCENE from D. W. Griffith's *Intolerance* is one of the monumentally large productions in motion-picture history. Hundreds of extras were used in the huge set. More important to the future of movies, *Intolerance* instituted the parallel or "cut-back" method of telling in turn several stories that all take place at the same time. (AMPAS)

AN AUTOGRAPHED PICTURE of Charles Chaplin, one of the film industry's earliest, most famous stars, who came to Los Angeles with Karno's English pantomime company, and stayed. Beginning with films like *Tillie's Punctured Romance,* directed by Mack Sennett and co-starring Marie Dressler, Chaplin went on to create his "Little Tramp" character and become one of the classic comedians in film history. (LA Title)

GRAND STATION was the Santa Fe terminal in Los Angeles in 1911. The architecture and decoration on the building suggest a Near Eastern influence. (LA Title)

THE LOS ANGELES TIMES BUILDING was reduced to rubble after a bombing on October 1, 1910. The incident, in which twenty-one employees were killed, came on the heels of an attempt by unions to establish themselves in the city. Union officials moved into Los Angeles when San Francisco Bay-area employers threatened to end cooperation if they were to be the only ones in the state. Strong opposition in Los Angeles was led by Harrison G. Otis, publisher of the *Times*. The unions were blamed for dynamiting the Times building, despite their contention that the blast was caused by a gas leak. James B. McNamara and his brother John, secretary of the International Association of Bridge and Structural Iron Workers' Union, were arrested, tried, and sentenced to life imprisonment. (LA Title)

THE FIRST AIRPLANE TO FLY in California
lands at the 1910 Dominguez Field Air Meet,
between Los Angeles and Long Beach. During
the meet, one of the earliest in the United
States, Louis Paulhan established a world's sus-
tained-flight record by flying his Bleriot mono-
plane forty-five miles to the Santa Anita Ranch
and back.

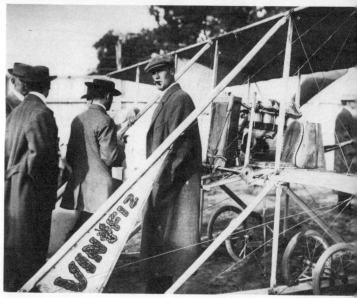

EARLY PILOT C. P. Rodgers chews his cigar
next to the biplane he flew cross-country to
Los Angeles in 1911 as a soft-drink promotion.
Arriving just before the New Year's Day Tournament of Roses, Rodgers was named king of
the event, and spent the day flying over the
parade dropping rose petals on the throngs.
(Roses)

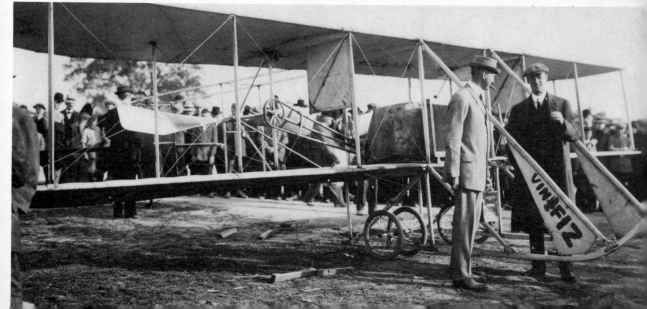

ANGEL'S FLIGHT, a cable railway, was a famous downtown Los Angeles tourist attraction in 1910, carrying passengers up the steep slopes of Bunker Hill between Hill and Olive streets to an observation tower one hundred feet above the Third Street tunnel. The top of the railway presented a panoramic view of the San Gabriel Mountains. It was built in 1901 by Col. J. W. Eddy. (LA Title)

THE LOS ANGELES POLICE became motorized law enforcers early in the twentieth century.

PUMPERS of the Los Angeles Fire Department found heavy action at the corner of Third and Broadway in 1913. (LA Title)

LADIES of the U. S. Post Office formed a rank in the 1916 Los Angeles Preparedness Day parade winding past the corner of Third and Broadway. (LA Title)

THE OWENS VALLEY PROJECT

bringing water to the Los Angeles area was a prodigious feat of engineering in its time. Hundreds of men worked to pour the tons of concrete that went into miles of ditches *(above)*. William Mulholland *(left),* chief engineer of the municipal Water Bureau, who found the Owens River 250 miles northeast of the city, was oneof the firecest campaigners in the battle over water rights in the Owens Valley. When the city won the fight, he was one of the prime movers in construction of the Aqueduct that brought the city its first water supply. For 133 years, the Los Angeles River had been the sole source of water for the growing town. Three large reservoirs were constructed along the route, and twelve miles of inverted steel siphons, twenty-four miles of open unlined conduit, thirty-nine miles of open cement conduit, and ninety-seven miles of covered conduit *(facing page, top)*. Teams of fifty-two mules *(below)*were used to haul single sections of the large conduit into position over the mountains. Special equipment, never to be used again, *(facing page, bottom)* was built to cut the 142 twisting tunnels that led the water through the hills. Work on the aqueduct started in 1907 and finished in 1913. (LADWP)

A FISHERMAN'S VILLAGE on Terminal Island in Los Angeles Harbor was mostly wood and tar paper about 1915. (SPNB)

THE LOS ANGELES RIVER, normally dry, went on a rampage during heavy rains of 1917, leaving helpless riverside residents to survey the damage to this house that slid into the riverbed when the stream undercut its banks. (SPNB)

CECIL B. DEMILLE, the world famous film director, flies his Curtiss Jenny bi-plane in a 1919 race with Eddie Hearne driving his Chevrolet racer. The race was conducted at Ascot Park Speedway in Los Angeles. Mechanic Harry Hartz rode with Hearne in the race. (Ronnie)

THE ENDLESS PIER at Redondo Beach was unique when built in 1916. A $125,000 marvel of concrete and steel, it included a pavilion restaurant, and a broad promenade with covered benches. Fishermen flocked there to catch the re-puted abundance of fish. But, within twenty months, a savage storm came ashore, shattering the concrete and twisting the steel reinforcement. The Endless Pier had to be abandoned as an engineering effort beyond the skills of its time. (CRB)

THE AMERICAN CLUB of Santa Ana leads a 1910 parade through the city. (LA Title)

SANTA ANA'S SCHOOLS combined student bodies to parade through the city in 1910, delighting their parents and passers-by. (LA Title)

NEWPORT BEACH was a collection of fashionable seaside cottages along Newport Bay during the second decade of the twentieth century. Following its founding in 1892, the city had a brief life as a commercial port but quickly lost its business traffic to San Pedro and other Pacific ports. The Santa Ana River-fed bay still retained its appeal for pleasure sailors, as it once had for Yankee smugglers. The city was to become the home of the largest pleasure-boat fleet on the Pacific Coast.

[177]

JOHN KNOX PORTWOOD and his burro freighting team was one of the most frequent users of the newly developed road through San Gabriel Canyon into the Antelope Valley around 1915.

COLORADO STREET and Fair Oaks Avenue in 1910 reflected Pasadena's calm. The city was founded by Dr. Thomas B. Elliott and friends from Indianapolis, Indiana, who formed the California Colony of Indiana "to get where life is easy."

ORANGE GROVE AVENUE in Pasadena was a busy mix of electric streetcars, early automobiles, and horse-drawn buggies in this 1910 picture.

TODAY'S HUNTINGTON LIBRARY and Art Gallery *(below)* in Pasadena was built as a home between 1910 and 1920 by millionaire Henry E. Huntington, who stands by the fountain. Huntington *(right)*, born in New York, came to San Francisco in 1892 to represent his uncle Collis P. Huntington in the Southern Pacific Railroad. He moved to Los Angeles following his uncle's death in 1902, where he became an important landowner and businessman. He retired at sixty to devote himself to art and literature. He executed the first deed to what would become the Huntington Library and Art Gallery in 1919. Since 1928, the institution has been open to the public.

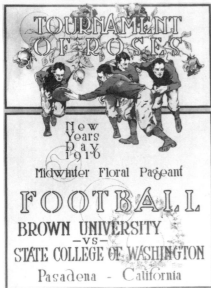

HARKENING TO THE DAYS of Roman grandeur, the chariot races were one of the highlights of Pasadena's annual Tournament of Roses in 1911. They climaxed the mid-winter festival of blossoms until well after the turn of the century.

THIS POSTER ADVERTISES the second football game associated with the Pasadena Tournament of Roses. The first one took place in 1902. Following that, other athletic activities were held during the festivities. Not until 1916 was it decided that football should be permanently associated with the festival. The Tournament that year lost $11,000 due to a heavy rainstorm that cut the crowd to 7,000 from a hoped-for 25,000. (Roses)

COLORADO STREET BRIDGE in Pasadena was opened October 13, 1913. The bridge across the dry bed of Arroyo Seco was curved in order to find suitable bedrock. A barbed-wire-topped fence was extended along the railing in 1937 to block the series of death leaps that gave the graceful bridge the nickname of "Suicide Bridge." The old structure is still in use.

THE PIER OF THE 100-INCH TELE-scope at the Mount Wilson Observatory under construction: Placement of the instrument that would increase the power of the human eye 250,000 times was well underway when this 1915 picture was taken.

THE SCRIPPS INSTITUTION OF Oceanography was the Scripp Institution of Biological Research when it joined the University of California in 1912. Located at La Jolla, just north of San Diego, the installation is next to the offshore La Jolla Trench and its wealth of oceanographic data. (SD Title)

THE STEAMSHIP *YALE* was an early Pacific Navigation Co. vessel carrying passengers up and down the California coast. What sea transportation meant to the coastal cities was demonstrated in 1910 when the *Yale* first stopped at San Diego, with 400 excursionists aboard. Cheers and whistles resounded from the wharfs. The ship's officers and passengers were taken around town in cars decked with the pennants of Harvard and Yale universities, the names of the steamship line's sister ships. When she sailed, a pilot from the Curtiss flying school bombarded the ship with oranges (SD Title)

JAPANESE NAVAL OFFICERS chat with American girls during a 1912 visit of their ship to San Diego. (SD Title)

MEMBERS OF THE ACME SOCIAL CLUB of San Diego gathered aboard the vessel *Grant* on March 1, 1917, to celebrate Gathern P. Perry's seventeenth birthday. The young celebrant is sitting in the bow holding a bouquet presented to him during the festivities. (SD Title)

THE U. S. GRANT HOTEL was opened in San Diego in 1910, in the flurry of activity that organized the Panama-California Exposition Co. The lavish $1,100,000 building contained $250,000 in furnishings. It was conceived by U. S. Grant, Jr., in memory of his father, and financed with the assistance of $700,000 in public subscriptions. The grand opening of the block-long structure attracted 500 visitors. (SD Title)

PILOT GLENN H. CURTISS, holding the card, and meteorologist Ford Carpenter, in the derby, meet with a Californian of an earlier era during a World War I-era air show at Dominguez Field. Possessing a faith in the future of aviation shared by few of his contemporaries, Curtiss arrived in San Diego in 1910 and established a flying school at North Island with the help of the Aero Club of San Diego and John D. Spreckels, a local civic leader, newspaper publisher, and millionaire. With his employee Eugene Ely, Curtiss pioneered military aviation. (SD Title)

AN EARLY AIRPLANE gets off the ground at a 1911 Coronado air meet with the aid of a few husky pushers. The plane is equipped with fuel tanks positioned for upsidedown flying. (SD Title)

THE CHILDREN of the theosophical school, Point Loma Homestead, in San Diego: The religious sect, the first of many that were to bring fame to Southern California, eventually owned approximately five hundred acres of land, and was given a warm welcome despite its views on reincarnation and other Orientally rooted beliefs. It was only a short time before it became controversial, with charges that the children, sent there from all over the world, were mistreated. Investigations proved that the boarding school, for all its deviationist teachings, was an immaculate institution. (SD Title)

FROST FORMED on the palm trees and ice collected on the fountain of the San Diego plaza on January 7, 1913, the coldest day ever recorded. The temperature dropped to 22 degrees in the normally balmy Southern California city. (SD Title)

STREETCARS were one of the dominant forms of transportation in San Diego along with horses, automobiles, and bicycles in the 1911 city. (SD Title)

SAN DIEGO POLICE turned fire hoses on International Workers of the World in 1913. Southern California received an influx of militant laborites and anarchists from all over the country after a group of them in the form of a rag-tag army failed in an attempt to conquer Baja California and establish their own government. Many of the radicals drifted to San Diego where they ranted on street corners in favor of the abolition of capitalism. There were not only clashes with the police. Citizens became increasingly irritated at the radicals, and, finally, anarchist leader Emma Goldman was chased from the city by a mob. The city soon returned to normal. (SD Title)

The Police Using Water on I.W.W's San Diego Cal. 1912

THE CALIFORNIA TOWER and the California Building dominated the Cabrillo Bridge entrance to San Diego's 1915 Panama-California Exposition in Balboa Park. Running slightly more than a year, the show hosted over two million visitors and paid all of its expenses. It was designed to celebrate the opening of the Panama Canal, and was supported by the United States and Spain. It attempted to reflect the history of the area and touted its attraction for the future as a major port. The Midway of the exposition *(below),* known as the Isthmus, also contained the rides and sideshows typical of such attractions. At this time San Diego had a population of 74,000. Six western states—Washington, Montana, Utah, Kansas, New Mexico, and Nevada—participated. (SD Title)

SAN DIEGO'S ornate old railroad station tower is pulled down to make way for a new one of Spanish-mission architecture compatible with the design of the 1915 Panama-California Exposition. The Santa Fe Railroad, which had occupied the old station, and the San Diego & Arizona Railway combined to construct the new station. (SD Title)

[187]

A JAUNTY CROWD of strikers walk out od San Diego High School and Junior College on June 6, 1918. The precise cause of the strike has been lost but it was apparently in response to the continuing stalemate on the World War I battlefields in France. (SD Title)

212 AIRPLANES from San Diego's Rockwell Field and other nearby military air bases took to the air November 27, 1918, to the awe of residents, atop city buildings to celebrate the end of World War I. The war was significant to San Diego because it marked the city's new relationship with the U. S. Navy. The Navy air arm had found a home at Rockwell Field, with 101 officers, 381 men and 497 planes there by the end of the war. (SD Title)

More Than Just Orange Trees: 1920 to 1930

WORLD WAR I, with its terrible casualties all across the country, scarred California as well. But in California people also talked of real estate deals that could be made, new tracts, new townships, new communities. And small boys loved the new streetcars.

So, by now, California had been blooded in at least three wars, it had been pierced by a highly controversial railway, it had suffered and enjoyed booms and busts, floods and foolishnesses. It was a magnet for folks who came to see more than "the elephant." "Seeing the elephant" was a Gold Rush expression with P. T. Barnum overtones. California had become much of what all the nation had become. A place with people. A melting pot in which the melted pieces never completely mixed—as in other states—and in which all residents, old and new, developed a totally irrational sense of boosterism that might have caused more headaches than pride.

HANCOCK LAKE lies in the Marble Mountain Wilderness of Klamath National Forest. The area near the state's northern border was heavily panned and mined during the mid-nineteenth century, but the nearly fifteen billion board-feet of sugar and ponderosa pine and Douglas fir have remained virtually untouched. The wing dams, stamp mills, dredges, and drift hydraulic mines of the gold rush still dot the area. (USFS)

A BIG-WHEEL LOG-WAGON TRAIN hauls logs out of Shasta National Forest about the turn of the century. Not suited to long travel over rough terrain, the large carts were used to bring the logs out of the woods to the railroad.

A LUMBER-CARRYING SHIP is loaded from the cliffs at Fort Bragg by means of a cable chute that carried the stacked lumber to the ship over the water. The system was in use until 1930. (Redwood)

THE HOUSE OF HAPPY WALLS, begun near Glen Ellen, Sonoma County, by author Jack London, was given its name by his widow, Mrs. Charmian London, It contains many mementos of the writer's travels and encounters, including a huge horseshoe made for him by World Heavyweight Champion Bob Fitz-simmons, an Australian blacksmith. London died five years before the building was completed in 1921. Today it is part of Jack London State Park. (Redwood)

PILOTS AT MATHER FIELD assemble on a DeHavilland DH-4 bi-plane for this 1920 photograph. The air base near Sacramento opened in 1918 as a pilot and navigator training installation. (MAFB)

[192]   THE TANKER *LYMAN STEWART* aground on the rocks at the entrance to San Francisco Bay: The 65,000-barrel ship was built in 1914 for Union Oil Co. simultaneously in a shipyard, with her sister ship, the *Frank N. Buck,* built for Associated Oil Co. Both went about their work until 1922, when the *Lyman Stewart* collided with another ship and was driven onto the rocks. Battered by surf for weeks, she finally broke up and sank. In 1937, her twin collided with the *President Coolidge* in the same spot, was driven onto the same rocks, and sank within fifty feet of where the *Stewart* rested. (UOC)

THE PALACE OF FINE ARTS, last remains of San Francisco's 1915 Panama-Pacific Exposition, stands on the shores of San Francisco Bay, where it housed an art collection throughout the three-year, $50,000,000 celebration. After the fair, the San Francisco Art Commission kept a collection there until 1921. The property was deeded to the city in 1927, but it took twelve years more to appropriate the $500,000 required to restore the crumbling Corinthian columns and the Roman rotunda. The palace currently houses tennis courts. (SFCVB)

THE SAN FRANCISCO LIBRARY of Ina D. Coolbrith depicted the ornate decor common to the city in the 1920s. (LA Title)

VAQUERO FELIPE AVILA poses in his finest togs for pictures immediately before the 1927 San Francisco Admission Day Parade. (LA Title)

WINCHESTER HOUSE in San Jose looks more like a residential development than one home. Built by Mrs. Sarah Winchester in her thirty-eight years there, the house had a solid-gold front-door key, 160 rooms, 10,000 windows, nine kitchens, forty-seven fireplaces, a forty-two-step staircase with two-inch steps, stairways that ended in blank walls, a second-story door opening out to nothing, and a hundred other oddities. Why did the heiress to the Winchester Repeating Arms millions build her now-famous house, why was the number 13 so prominent in the design? Some believed that she communed with a spirit world that promised she would never die as long as construction continued. Whatever the reason, Mrs. Winchester built from her arrival there in 1884 until her death in 1922. (Winchester)

A SUMMER DAY in downtown Fresno around 1929: The growth of the agricultural center of the San Joaquin Valley into a city with tall buildings and modern automobiles, is suggested here, as well as an air of lamppost-leaning conversations that the valley's heat often induces. (SPNB)

PRES. AND MRS. HERBERT HOOVER met welcoming crowds during a visit to Santa Barbara in the late 1920s. Among those greeting the president were Bernard Hoffman, extreme right, and Mrs. Hoffman, standing to the right of Mrs. Hoover. (SPNB)

EARTHQUAKE DAMAGE is apparent on the facade of Santa Barbara's Arlington Hotel. The famous old hotel was near the northern edge of the June 29, 1925, earthquake's damage zone. The shock left much heavier damage along the city's main street. (SPNB)

AN EASTER SUNRISE SERVICE IN DEATH VALLEY: Such religious services in the midst of the valley's desolation were common during the 1920s.

DEATH VALLEY SCOTTY, hat on knee, sits in his desert home, Scotty's Castle, with his partners Mr. and Mrs. Albert M. Johnson. Probably the most famous Death Valley prospector, Scotty was a spinner of tall tales with Buffalo Bill's Wild West Show. He became a darling of the press. On a well-publicized rail trip to Chicago, Scotty met Johnson and so enamored him with the desert that the businessman built a $2,000,000 "castle" near Scotty. The desert prospector, known as a lavish spender, never had visible means of income. They say he conned normally hardheaded businessmen to invest in his gold-mining company. He termed these men his "rootin' section."

FORDING A STREAM was not a rare experience for the pioneer California motorist. Here state workers drag cars across a swollen stream. (CDPW)

ENGLISH WALNUTS LAID OUT FOR CLEANING AND DRYING: Since the turn of the century, California trees have produced the vast majority of the walnuts in the United States.

BEAUTIFUL DOWNTOWN BURBANK: The view of the main artery through Burbank, San Fernando Road, was taken in 1927. In the middle of the block, in the middle of the picture, there is a traffic cop. Later came traffic signals, "Laugh In," and a freeway that protects Burbank from the north-south traffic that once clogged this street. (SPNB)

GLENDALE'S BRAND BOULEVARD was a bustling business thoroughfare at the time of this 1926 picture. The Glendale Theatre, right, offered residents five vaudeville acts daily. (LA Title)

THE 364TH INFANTRY receives a tumultuous welcome home in 1920 when the troops returned to Los Angeles from service in World War I. (SPNB)

PASADENA'S BUSCH GARDENS in this 1920s picture is seventy-five acres of formal gardens, natural woods, and a maze of paths. Strollers were entertained by terracotta gnomes and elves arranged in scenes from Hans Christen Anderson's and Grimm's fairytales. The gardens were from the estate of St. Louis brewer, A. H. Busch, who took a significant interest in Los Angeles affairs.

PILOT-STUNTMAN OMAR Locklear knocks the church steeple off for the Universal film *The Sky-wayman.* Arriving in Los Angeles in 1919, Locklear gained an immediate reputation for his wing walking and changing planes in mid-air. The stunt shown here did little damage to the plane despite the apparent disaster. Film-makers, impressed, hired him for *The Winged Trail,* featuring him and Francilla Billington. On the night of August 2, 1920, he flew over Hollywood when a movie required him to tail spin from 2,000 feet while held in the beam of a searchlight. Blinded by the lights, he crashed in the Fairfax-Melrose area. Both he and his frequent passenger, Skeets Elliott, were killed. (NIT)

OMAR LOCKLEAR stands on his head during a 1920s flight over Beverly Hills. The farmland and sparse oil derricks are in sharp contrast to the fashionable homes there today. (Ronnie-Locklear)

TWENTIES SILLINESS: California suffered its share of publicity-seeking silliness sessions. This elephant-scrubbing scene is how some Beverly Hill ladies helped to promote their 1927 Beverly Hills Society Circus. The elephant loved it. (SPNB)

ROGERS AND DEMILLE NO. 2 airports were separated by Wilshire Boulevard and Fairfax Avenue, which ran through open farmland at the time of this 1921 picture. The area is now one of heavy urbanization. (Ronnie)

A FORD TRIMOTOR passenger plane unloads Los Angeles bound passengers. The passenger flight is met at the airport by one of the double-decker Pickwick Stage motorcoaches used in Southern California in 1929. (SPNB)

RECORD-SETTING PILOT Wiley Post, like many early pilots, was in and out of Southern California regularly. When Carl Squiers, of Lockheed, and Ray Boggs organized Nevada Airlines in 1929, Post became one of the line's pilots. Despite all of the records he recorded on the side of his famous plane "The Winnie Mae," Post's most famous flight was his greatest failure. In 1935, he and humorist Will Rogers were killed when their plane crashed in the Alaskan wilderness.

DOUGLAS AIRCRAFT COMPANY'S Santa Monica Plant in the 1920s was a primitive operation set in the open fields and sparse residential area common at that time around Clover Field, Santa Monica's municipal airport. Established in 1926, the field was one of the Los Angeles area's earliest municipal airports and one of the first anywhere in the U. S. From its runway, Amelia Earhart, Charles Lindberg, Howard Hughes and other aviation pioneers made many of their flights. The firm maintained its offices in Santa Monica despite its growth to international fame during and after World War II. (Douglas)

A DOUGLAS AIRCRAFT CLOUDSTER is serviced in Los Angeles before its flight for Los Angeles-San Diego Air Line. The first plane designed by famous aircraft pioneer Donald Douglas for his own firm, the plane first took to the air in Santa Monica on February 24, 1921. It was the first plane with the ability to lift a useful load greater than its own weight. (Douglas)

A DOUGLAS AIRCRAFT DT TORPEDO BOMBER in its commercial version flies past a freighter. The plane was developed in 1921, and a Navy order in late 1922 for a total of 41 planes put the firm on a paying basis for the first time. The first three DTs had been constructed by Donald Douglas and twenty employees. They were completely hand-made. (Douglas)

THIS STRANGE BIRD was one of the Southern California aircraft developments that did not result in an industrial giant, a 1929 combination helicopter, ornithopter, and airplane. The Los Angeles inventor's plan was for the wings to flap and the twin rotors on top were expected to add to the lift. The front propeller drove it forward. The craft even had a unique spring-loaded landing gear. As far as is known. it never got off the ground. (NIT)

THE GARDENS around the Ramona Verdugo home, one of California's early Spanish pioneers, make a pleasant setting for these 1921 visitors. (LA Title)

AIMEE SEMPLE McPHERSON founded her Four Square Gospel in Los Angeles in 1923. Religion, including Japanese and Chinese temples, had always been an important factor in the community's development. In the early 1900s the town had 231 churches with more than eighty thousand members. Religion blossomed in the prosperity of post-World War I America. Aimee Semple McPherson's spectacular, and somewhat theatrical, group at Angelus Temple soon attracted up to forty thousand members.

[204]

In addition to its $2,000,000 temple, the sect founded a Bible college, branch churches, and missions throughout the world. Partly because of the woman evangelist's success, other religious cults picked Southern California as their base. The influx became so massive that a Columbia University professor declared that Los Angeles County had a branch of every religion in the world, and a few not known anywhere else in the world. (SPNB)

THE MIDWAY of Venice Amusement Park was filled with thrilling rides, souvenir shops, and gaming stalls in 1924. The Ship Cafe, where many Hollywood personalities could be found, was tied up between the roller coaster rides. One of the major attractions of the Southern California copy of the Italian city was that it was one of the few "wet" towns during Prohibition. (SPNB)

THE BROADWAY TUNNEL on the Pacific Electric interurban streetcar line was considered an oddity when it was opened for service to Los Angeles in 1926. (SPNB)

AN EARLY MILK DELIVERYMAN goes about his daily rounds in a Los Angeles not yet dominated by the automobile. (SPNB)

LOS ANGELES POLICE examine an illegal still discovered during national Prohibition. (SPNB)

PACIFIC ELECTRIC RAILWAY CO. feeder-bus driver Russell L. Leadabrand and bus No. 55 pause along Allen Avenue in 1927. The motor buses brought residents of Pasadena to the interurban streetcar terminals in the city for transport to Los Angeles and elswhere. Drivers of these poorly exhausted buses often became ill from the fumes, fumes that one day would be measured as contributory to the Southern California smog problem. In 1931, Leadabrand turned in his cap, left the exhausts of No. 55, and became a gentleman farmer in a smogless (and busless) part of the state.

LON CHANEY, "The Man of 1,000 Faces," one of the most famous stars of the early Hollywood film industry, pauses to stitch a rip in his castaway costume for the 1923 film *All the Brothers Were Valiant*. Chaney and other members of the cast spent five weeks aboard the whaling schooner *Carolyn Frances* preparing for the movie. Chaney became world-famous for his role in the *Hunchback of Notre Dame* and other parts, in which he became a master of makeup and disguise. (AMPAS)

PROBABLY THE EARLIEST WESTERN HERO of the American film industry was William S. Hart. In this picture, Hart is costumed for his role in the 1925 production of *Tumbleweeds*. During his career, Hart was in numerous films, setting the tone of Western heroes to come. (AMPAS)

RADIO STATION KFI, along with KNX and KHJ, went on the air in 1922 as the first stations in the Los Angeles area. As in most parts of the country, they had spotty success in their early days. KNX started as a promotion for the *Los Angeles Express* and succeeded so well that it was kept on the air. KFI was begun to promote a new car dealership, and KHJ was started by the *Los Angeles Times*. All three later joined nationwide networks and became the dominant radio voices in the area. Here, the announcer works at a table with an ancient set of Westinghouse receivers in the background. (KFI-LA)

ONE OF THE EARLIEST PORTABLE RADIOS is shown off by a California mermaid. (SPNB)

THE ST. FRANCIS DAM was the terminus of the Los Angeles-Owens Valley aqueduct until March 13, 1928. That night, the dam in San Francisquito Canyon, broke without warning. A wall of water swept down the canyon, smashing houses and killing approximately six hundred persons. Ten bridges, several miles of highway, part of the aqueduct system, a power plant, several hundred homes, and ten thousand acres of farm crops were destroyed in minutes. William Mulholland, one of the chief drivers behind the dam's construction, was emotionally shattered when he was notified of the disaster. (LADWP)

THE 20TH CENTURY-FOX STUDIOS in Beverly Hills was one of the largest movie plants in the world. The first movie studio was erected behind a Chinese laundry on Olive Street in 1908 after Francis Boggs came to Laguna Beach to complete the shooting of the single reel verson of *The Count of Monte Cristo.* They were soon followed by other moviemakers fleeing lawsuits filed by Thomas A. Edison over the patents on his film inventions. The battle between the film "pirates" and the so-called "trust" (the film-makers who had been licensed by Edison) continued after both groups wound up in the rolling Hollywood Hills. The main 20th Century-Fox studio is in the upper portion of the photograph. That area housed the seven soundproof stages, the dressing rooms, and the administration buildings. The lower two-thirds of the plant contained three more stages, a mill and garage, the outdoor street scenes of the "back lot." Here, on the lower edge is the New York street scene, with its brick buildings and elevated train. To the left of New York, is the tunnel set for *East River,* and just above that is the New England street where *David Harum* was filmed. (AMPAS)

THE NAVY DIRIGIBLE *Shenandoah* appeared in the skies over Los Angeles for the first time on October 16, 1924, en route from San Diego to Camp Lewis, Washington. The junket was part of a cross country flight from Lakehurst, New Jersey that saw the giant lighter-than-air ship log 8,100 miles and 258.38 flying hours. The *Shenandoah* reappeared in the Los Angeles sky for the last time October 21, 1924, on her return from Camp Lewis. The Vaught bi-plane that joined the ship over Southern California is a dramatic demonstration of the ship's massive 680-foot length. She was seventy-nine feet in diameter and was powered by five Packard 300 horsepower engines. (NIT)

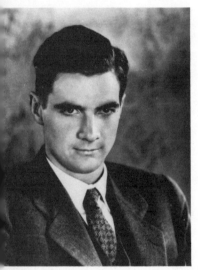

INDUSTRIALIST HOWARD HUGHES started his aviation career in 1926 when he thought of producing an epic film based on World War I aviation. He learned to fly at the American Aircraft flying school at Mines Field, which later became Los Angeles International Airport, and soloed in August, 1927 at American Airport on Crenshaw Boulevard. His initial contribution to aviation was production of the film *Hells Angels* which employed 72 pilots and 65 mechanics for two years. He later set several records for long distance flying and was instrumental in many aircraft design innovations and the development of commercial air travel. He was the driving force behind the creation of Trans World Airlines and later Hughes Air West. (NIT)

CHARLIE CHAPLIN, right, poses with film stars Mildred Harris, Mary Pickford, Marjorie Daw, Miss Pickford's niece, and Douglas Fairbanks at DeMille Airport in 1920. Like many other Hollywood personalities of that day, the group were flying enthusiasts. Fairbanks and Pickford, known as "America's Sweethearts," were one of the nation's most famous married couples. At the time of this picture, Miss Harris and Chaplin were married. (AMPAS)

YOUNG LADIES at Redondo Beach show off their beauty as well as the latest in fashion during this 1924 fashion show. (CRB)

JUAN SEGUNDO, a Coahuilla Indian at Torres, east of Palm Springs, was captured by the camera in this 1920s photograph—an extraordinary picture and an extraordinary face. (LA Title)

CITY OFFICIALS and businessmen in Los Angeles await their party on the first telephone connection from the West Coast city to London. (SPNB)

SIGNAL HILL OILFIELD, near Long Beach, was the richest oil strike per acre in the world when it was discovered in 1921. By the end of the year, there were five hundred derricks on the site, and by the end of 1923, there were more than one thousand derricks on a spot no more than two square miles in size. With an average production of almost two hundred fifty thousand barrels a day, the field's attraction tripled the population of Long Beach, doubled the shipping using the Panama Canal, and turned the entire area into a greasy forest of derricks. Still a major oilfield, Signal Hill produced more than four hundred million barrels of oil in its first decade. (Burmah)

"THE LITTLE GIANT OF SIGNAL HILL," Sam Mosher, stands on a drill platform in the Signal Hill oilfield. Although the first wildcat well was drilled by Royal Dutch Shell, Mosher's was one of the better-known success stories to come out of the fabulous oil strike. Recognizing most oilmen's disinterest in the "wet gas" that forced the oil to the surface, he borrowed $4,000 from his father, built a natural gasoline absorption plant, and parlayed his investment into a five-million-dollar company. Signal Gasoline Company later became the Signal Companies, Incorporated, with assets of $1.3 billion. (Burmah)

HEAVY AUTOMOBILE TRAFFIC would become the hallmark of Southern California in the mid-twentieth century. It was already well along in its development by the time of this mid-1920s picture of the Pacific Coast highway adjacent to Santa Monica Bay. (CDPW)

THE SPRAWLING UCLA CAMPUS in Los Angeles consisted of only four buildings and a quadrangle when it was opened in 1929. Surrounding the quad, from the lower left clockwise, were Royce Hall, the Chemistry Building, the Physics-Biology Building, and the Powell Library. With the quad as its center, the campus later expanded over the filled-in arroyo above the original campus. (UCLA)

SANTA CATALINA ISLAND, twenty-six miles off the Southern California coast, was discovered by the earliest Spanish explorers. The twenty-two-mile-long island served as a Russian sea otter hunting base in 1811, and later a base for smuggling foreign goods to the California mainland. Gold was discovered on the island in 1834, but not exploited until 1863, when American prospectors drove their mines from the island under the seabed. The island was evacuated during the Civil War for fear that Confederates would use it as a base for privateering in the Pacific. The island's one and only city, Avalon, lies at the mouth of a canyon opening onto a crescent-shaped bay. Catalina became a commercial success after it was purchased by chewing gum magnate William Wrigley Jr. He put on one of the most extensive publicity campaigns in California to get tourists to the island. The island is noted for its outstanding fishing, its quaint city, and the beauty of its mountain-ribbed back country. The pebbly beaches front on placid bays ideal for swimming and water sports. In this 1920s picture, the ship that served the island regularly for many years, the *S. S. Catalina,* is coming into port among the many pleasure boats on Avalon Bay. (SPNB)

[214]

MODERN COLLECTORS of antique cars would go mad if turned loose on this 1920s main street in Anaheim. Obviously made painstakingly with a fine camera, this photograph has an uncommonly good depth of field and sharpness. The street is decked with flags for an upcoming summer parade, and Daley's Groceries has boxes of California produce for sale in front of the shop. (LA Title)

THE ROSE BOWL was built in 1922 at an original cost of $272,198.26. The original stadium was a horseshoe with a 57,000 seating capacity. The open-end stadium was later closed to form the bowl, and the seating capacity was expanded to 100,000. (Roses)

THE MOST FAMOUS PLAY in Rose Bowl history took place during the 1929 football game between California and Georgia Tech. The play started when Tech's "Stumpy" Thomason made a nice gain around left end only to fumble when he was tackled. The loose ball bounced into the hands of California center Roy Riegels at the Yellow Jacket 35-yard line. Riegels ran for the Tech goal. En route, he wheeled to duck a tackle, got confused, and started running toward his own goal line, despite the shouts of his own teammates. They finally stopped him after he reached his one-yard line. After California's punt was blocked that close to the goal, Georgia Tech was awarded a safety and won the game. (Roses)

THE SOUTH PASADENA OSTRICH
farm, in the 1920s, was one of several such
farms established as both amusement parks
and to grow plumage around the turn of the
century. The first of the farms was started
in 1885 by a Dr. Sketchlye, a natural historian. He opened his farm as an amusement
center and did a thriving business. Other
farms were established during the next two
decades. Opened originally for amusement
and to inform the public like other zoos,
the farms did a thriving business in ostrich
plumes when women's fashions began to demand them. The large disc in the center of
this photograph contains a mirror to inten-
sify the heat and light, to produce the
temperature conditions of the birds'
African homelands.

THE HOTEL AND BEACH at Del Mar were popular attractions in the rollicking days of 1929 before the stock market collapsed. The Hotel Del Mar on the site was the second that attempted to survive at the resort. The first, built during one of the land booms of the late eighteenth century, burned shortly after it became apparent that the area would not be developed immediately. (SD Title)

WORLD-FAMOUS AVIATOR Eddie Rickenbacker drives past one of the Torrey pines. The trees, growing along the cliffs between La Jolla and Del Mar, are a rare variety known only to this spot and to Santa Rosa Island of the Channel Island group off Santa Barbara. The twisted, gnarled trees are the last relics of forests that grew in a very different climate and soil. Long before this 1920 picture was taken, San Diego officials and several wealthy residents had acquired much of the pine stand for preservation. (SD Title)

JAPANESE ADMIRAL H. SATO is flanked by his aide and a Japanese official during his 1928 visit to San Diego. (SD Title)

[217]

FIRST TRANSATLANTIC PILOT Charles A. Lindbergh came to San Diego to pick up the *Spirit of St. Louis,* his plane, for the hop to Paris. The 25-year-old airmail pilot began to consider the flight for the $25,000 prize during the winter of 1926-1927, after seeing an ad for a new monoplane being built by San Diego's Ryan Airlines. Once the tests of the new plane satisfied him, the "Lone Eagle" spent several weeks in San Diego working with designer T. Claude Ryan, airline owner B. Franklin Mahoney, and plant foreman Fred H. Rohr. When both he and the plane were ready, Lindbergh flew his long-range plane from San Diego to New York to begin the flight that would make him a legend. (Lockheed)

NAVY FIGHTERS parked at North Island Air Station in the 1920s were a mere hint at the massive air armadas that would fight through the Pacific in a few years, and the San Diego area's deep involvment in naval air and surface activities in the future. Most of the fighter aircraft in this picture are Curtiss F6C biplanes, with a few other models mixed with them. (USN)

[218]

THE U. S. S. *Langley* tied up at San Diego's North Island Naval Air Station: The Navy's first experimental aircraft carrier became a common sight around San Diego Bay as airplanes became a new dimension in sea warfare. The *Langley* was the only carrier to visit North Island when this photo was taken in 1924, but by 1927, city and military officials were dredging a deeper turning basin to handle the U. S. S. *Lexington, Saratoga,* and other giant carriers that would fight World War II. (USN)

THE SAN DIEGO BUSINESS DISTRICT, along Sixth Street from Beech, was a bustling area in 1929.
(SD Title)

THE UNITED STATES-MEXICO BORDER CROSSING at San Ysidro in 1927 was already undergoing heavy automobile traffic. (SD Title)

THE FERRYBOAT *Silver Gate* was the primary method of getting from San Diego to Coronado Island before the construction of the bay bridge in the mid-twentieth century. (SD Title)

HISTORIC HOTEL DEL CORONADO was constructed on the Pacific side of San Diego Bay's Coronado Island as part of a land development speculation during one of the land booms of the 1880s. Railroad financier Elisha Babcock, of Evansville, Indiana, was the prime mover in the project, selling lots on the island to pay for the hotel's construction. He ordered a ferryboat to connect the hotel to the mainland side of the bay and started a nationwide advertising campaign that brought settlers and made the hotel world-famous. The hotel hosted Edward, Prince of Wales *(right)*, in 1920 during a reception for the officers of visiting warship H. M. S. *Renown*. The prince reputedly met Mrs. Wallis Warfield, wife of a junior American naval officer, at a social gathering. He was only one of many distinguished visitors the hotel has entertained in its history. (USN-SD Title)

AN AIR MAIL INVITATION for Pres. Franklin D. Roosevelt to visit Northern California's Redwood Country is prepared for delivery from San Francisco in the 1930s. The invitation was carved on a redwood burl. (Redwood)

IRVIN S. COBB stands next to a giant Coast Redwood near Eureka that was named for him. (Redwood)

CALIFORNIA WESTERN RAILWAY'S "Skunk Line" got its nickname from the smell emitted by its steam locomotives and later its diesel tram cars on the forty miles of winding track from Willits to Fort Bragg in northwest California. The railroad acknowledged this reputation and painted a skunk on the sides of its cars. (Redwood)

The Great Depression: 1930 to 1940

ALL THE CALAMITIES of the Great Depression—soup kitchens and unemployment— were suffered in the Golden State, but again the climate attracted the homeless and the drought-weary; attracted them and gave them a new home.

Again, it was California's unquenchable vitality that had something to do with the migrations that began and continued even after the Dust Bowl days. John Steinbeck tells of some of the thoughts of the migrant fruit workers in the Depression in *In Dubious Battle*. California knew numerous CCC Camps, WPA projects, and NYA college students. The Depression settled on California, but when it was over, California seemed to shrug off the blue mood and move ahead once again. Often, again, in a cockeyed manner.

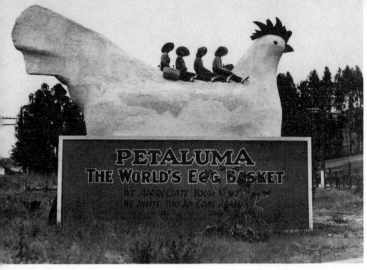

THE CITY OF PETALUMA was proud of its position as egg producer for the nation in the 1930s. The huge chicken with its cargo of pretty girls was constructed for one of the city's annual Egg Festivals. (Redwood)

THIS SERBIAN CHURCH near Jackson in Calaveras County served one of the more unusual minorities that settled in California's Mother Lode Country.

WORKERS at the historic Beringer Brothers Napa Valley Wine Press in 1934: The three-story stone building is one of the historic sites in the wine-grape country. Included in the photograph are Arthur Beringer, left front; Frederick Beringer; Martha Beringer, sixth from the left; and Bertha Beringer, second from the right. (Redwood)

P-12 FIGHTER PLANES OF THE 20TH PURSUIT GROUP get a going over from mechanics on the Mather Field flight line in the early 1930s. The group was organized at the California base in 1930 and remained there until 1932. Major Clarence Tinker, later the first Army Air Force general killed in World War II, commanded the group during its Mather stay. (MAFB)

A NAVY UO-1 AZTEC biplane approaches the flight deck of one of the Navy's pre-World War II blimps. The frame fixed to the top of the plane was designed to mate with the metal scaffolding extending from the lighter-than-air ship. Once the two were locked together, the plane could be hoisted inside the huge blimp. (USN)

THE GOLDEN GATE BRIDGE stands on its twin towers across the mouth of San Francisco Bay. Completed in 1937, the 8,940-foot-long bridge—the longest in the world at the time of its opening—has a center span of 4,200 feet between its towers. The towers stand 746 feet above high tide, the height of a 65-story building. To construct the foundation for the south tower, in the swirling currents common at that point, workmen operated from barges frequently tossed by fifteen-foot swells. They built concrete fenders down to bedrock and sunk caissons inside the fenders. With that completed, and the towers in place, workmen clambered on catwalks as they spun the 36.5 inch cables that support the structure. The towers of the "bridge that could never be built" support a 210-million-pound vertical load. The shore anchors can withstand a pull of 63 million pounds. The span is 220 feet above low water, permitting the passage of almost any ship. Fort Point National Historic Site stands under the bridge's shoreline anchors. The fort was one of the construction bases for the project. (NPS)

WORKERS CLING TO SAFETY NETS as they build the Golden Gate Bridge in 1937. Shortly before the bridge was completed, a scaffold car fell from the structure, tore the net, and eleven men were killed. (Redwood)

TOWERS OF THE GOLDEN GATE BRIDGE rise over San Francisco Bay in this photograph. In the lower right corner, historic Fort Point was the center of the construction operation. (Redwood)

ALCATRAZ ISLAND stands menacingly in the midst of San Francisco Bay. From 1859 to 1933 the island that would acquire the evil nickname "The Rock," was a military prison and an Army disciplinary barracks. Turned over to the federal prison system, Alcatraz became the home of the nation's most unruly and incorrigible prisoners. The island was considered escape-proof because of the swift currents that swirl around it. Two prisoners made the attempt in 1938 and were never heard from again. The prison was notorious for its rigid discipline and control over the convicts. It had an "electric eye" to detect metal on prisoners as they went about their tasks. Convicts were permitted to have visitors only with the warden's permission. Before the United States gained control of California, the infamous island was fortified for the Spanish defense of San Francisco Bay. (SFVB)

[227]

SAN FRANCISCO BAY and Alcatraz Island provide a scenic background for the California Street cable car in this 1930s photograph.

SITE OF THE UNITED NATIONS CHARTER signing, San Francisco's War Memorial Opera House was opened in 1932, after years of political wrangling. For the opening of the 3,285-capacity building, world-famous Lily Pons sang *Tosca*. It was the only municipally-owned opera house in the nation at the time of its opening. Located in the city's Civic Center, the Opera House is the home of the local symphony orchestra and opera company. (SFCVB)

A REFLECTING POOL on the grounds of the 1939 San Francisco exposition was an attractive setting for visitors to the show. (LA Title)

THE PERMANENTE CEMENT PLANT, on the banks of Permanente Creek near San Jose, became the cornerstone of Kaiser Cement and Gypsum Corporation. The *Saturday Evening Post* described the plant as "close to perpetual motion as Kaiser has come so far." A large shovel up the mountain loads a two-mile conveyor belt with six tons of gravel at a time. The conveyor moves down the mountain to the plant by gravity. Its brakes generate the power required to harvest the limestone. (Kaiser)

THE WAWONA TUNNEL TREE in Yosemite National Park was visited in 1935 by Park Superintendent Col. Charles G. Thomson, left front; National Park Service Assistant Supervisor Frank Ewing; and, left to right, Mrs. Thomson, a Mrs. Berry and Mrs. Ewing. The road was cut through the 231-foot tree in 1880 after Congress gave the 752,744 acre valley of 429 lakes and mountains to the state of California as a state park. The federal government took the land back for a national park in 1890, and Yosemite State Park was incorporated into it. The region was guarded by federal troops and civilian rangers until the formation of the National Park Service in 1916. (NPS)

AUTOMOBILE EXPLORATION OF DEATH VALLEY was still a new and daring passtime in the 1930s.

A SOLITARY DESERT DWELLER *(above),* one of a breed of men who have inhabited California's arid interior since the gold rush, didn't see any reason to change his method of getting from place to place, despite the invasion of the automobile.

JIM MYERS *(right)* waits in the door of his Priest Valley cabin for one of the deer that were still plentiful in the area at the time of this 1939 picture. (Myers)

THE TONOPAH & TIDEWATER RAILROAD still served California's eastern deserts in the 1930s. Originally constructed by Pacific Coast Borax Company to carry ore, the trains quickly became the basic general service transportation in much of the desert.

ARROYO SECO was little more than a usually-dry watercourse running from the foot of the San Gabriel Mountains to the Los Angeles River at the time of this 1933 picture. The shrubbery-choked ravine was occupied by a few shanties and some city parks that provided refuge for wildlife in the area. The arroyo was periodically the drainage basin for heavy rains washing off the mountains. It would eventually become the route of the nation's first freeway. (CDPW)

A 20-MULE TEAM revisits the ruins of the Harmony Borax Works in 1934. Designed by John W. S. Perry, the 100-foot long mule teams and their wagons were the ideal solution to desert transportation. Borax wagons had wheels seven feet in diameter on the rear and five feet in diameter in front. They were shod with steel tires eight inches wide and an inch thick. The sixteen-foot long wagons, and their six-foot deep and four-foot wide beds, weighed 7,800 pounds empty and 31,800 full. From Mojave to Harmony was a 166-mile, 20-day trip across the desert and through the Panamint Mountains. Temperatures of 130 degrees were not unusual. The teams really consisted of 18 mules and two horses, placed at the wheel positions because of their strength and obedience. A single jerk line tied to the bit of the left mule passed through rings in the harness to the driver, who either sat on the lead wagon or rode the left wheelhorse. A system of jerk signals told the lead mule when and which way to turn. The length of the mule train required that the animals be highly trained to keep the wagons in the roads on turns. If all of them pulled in the direction of a turn, the wagons would be dragged across it. Three teams were trained to jump across the tracechain that ran through the hitch and pull in the opposite direction. When the turn was done, they had to jump back over the chain and begin their straight pull again. No wonder the skinners were described as solarity, short-tempered men.

THE U.S.S. *Harvard* was one of the "floating palaces" carrying passengers along the Pacific Coast until May 30, 1931, when she went aground on the rocks of Point Arguello, north of Santa Barbara, in heavy fog. The five hundred passengers were taken off the cruise ship in lifeboats, transferred to the Navy cruiser *Louisville,* and evacuated to San Pedro. The *Harvard* was lost on the same rocks that had claimed a flotilla of seven Navy destroyers in 1923. (SD Title)

BEALE'S CUT or Fremont Pass on the Ridge Route from Los Angeles to San Joaquin Valley was so steep that horse-drawn wagons had their wheels chained before starting down the grade. With the teams stepping slowly and carefully, the bound wheels provided some braking as they skidded over the rocky road. Automobiles had it easier-but not by much. (CDPW)

THE DE LA GUERRA FAMILY gathers at Santa Barbara in 1930 in traditional Spanish dress and American military uniforms. (LA Title)

THE PORTAL OF THE LOS ANGELES COLISEUM was the entrance to the Xth Olympiad in 1932. The idea of bringing the games to the city started in 1912, when Fred Kelly, a local youth, won the 110-meter hurdles in Stockholm. The state, and especially its southern cities, had been holding annual celebrations for several years in an effort to attract residents, as for instance the Tournament of Roses and La Fiesta de Los Angeles. The suggestion was first made at the 1919 meeting of the California Fiestas Association. Colonel William M. Garland, a local financier, went to Europe with the invitation and plans for a new stadium to meet with the International Olympic Committee. Since the VIIIth and IXth games had already been allocated, Garland had to wait until 1924, when Los Angeles was picked for the 1932 games. As the games approached, the Great Depression combined with lack of knowledge about the United States by many Europeans caused some consternation. Many were shocked to learn that it was a long trip from New York to the West Coast. One group of Cuban athletes went home when they arrived in Galveston, Texas, and found out that Los Angeles was not a suburb of the Gulf Coast town. (LA Title)

[233]

THE GAMBLING SHIP *Johanna Smith* was one of several such vessels that anchored just outside the jurisdiction of federal authorities along the California coast in the 1920s and 1930s. Fast launches ran to and from piers in Santa Monica, Redondo Beach, Long Beach, San Pedro, San Diego, and other coastal cities, carrying pleasure seekers. In some spots, passenger trains ran directly to the wharves, unloading riders only a few steps from their boats. The *Johanna Smith* stood off the Long Beach-San Pedro area. The economic decline of the 1930s, and the threat of enemy naval attack with the beginning of World War II, put an end to the floating gambling spas. (LA Title)

THE GAMBLING S.S. *Monte Carlo* did not have to wait for the Depression and World War II to put it out of business—it ran aground off San Diego instead. (SD Title)

A LONE GUARD stands vigil over the rubble of a Compton business-district block following the devastating earthquake of March 10, 1933. (SPNB)

EARTHQUAKE DAMAGE left in the wake of a 1933 tremor that struck Long Beach is being inspected by Gov. James Rolph Jr. and a delegation of state and local officials. (SPNB)

SOUP LINES formed in many California cities during the Great Depression of the 1930s. Here, unemployed persons receive soup and sandwiches in front of the Los Angeles Plaza Church. Church workers pass out food purchased from Sunday collection funds. (SPNB)

OLD MAN DEPRESSION is done in by a group of pretty girls swinging a pick during a 1930s Valley of the Moon Jubilee at Glen Ellen. The celebration, held over the Labor Day weekend, was dedicated to ending the economic depression. (Redwood)

LOS ANGELES RESTAURANTS became an art form all their own in the decade before World War II. As the city grew and became more cosmopolitan, eating places both plain and fancy sought public attention through the shape of their buildings as well as the quality of their food. (SPNB)

TRAFFIC SPEEDS ALONG THE PASADENA FREEWAY, the first freeway in the United States, in this 1939 picture. At the time the road was constructed, the maximum speed limit in the state was forty-five miles per hour. Later increases in the speed limit did not change the freeway's forty-five-per-hour engineering. It soon became a "slow" member of the freeway system. (CDPW)

TRAFFIC INVESTIGATION was already becoming an important segment of California law enforcement in the 1930s. Here, members of an early Pasadena Police Department traffic investigation unit displays its equipment before going on duty. Many of the tools of modern criminology, the camera and lighting equipment were already in use. (PPD)

CALIFORNIA SERVICE STATIONS went to almost any lengths to make themselves look different and get the driving public's attention during the 1930s. (SPNB)

THE EDWARD L. DOHENY, JR., MEMORIAL LIBRARY dominated University of Southern California campus in the mid-1930s. Built on land donated by a Protestant, a Catholic, and a Jew, the formerly Methodist school was declared non-sectarian in 1926. The library, modeling the Romanesque style of the pre-World War II buildings on the campus, was built at a cost of $1,105,000, by oil magnate Edward L. Doheny, who first discovered oil in Los Angeles and was allegedly involved in the Tea Pot Dome scandal of the 1920s. Despite the economic depression in the United States, the student body had grown to several thousand by the 1930s. (USC)

HEAVYWEIGHT CHAMPION Jack Dempsey, standing in the leading car, is the object of a parade during a Los Angeles visit. (SPNB)

PIONEER WOMAN PILOT Amelia Earhart talks with (from left) Allan Lockhhed, Carl Squier, and Lloyd Stearman, during a 1932 visit to a Lockheed Aircraft hangar in Burbank, California. A native of Achison, Kansas, Miss Earhart served as a nurse for World War I soldiers and later studied at Columbia University. She came to California after dropping out of the university, and worked to pay for her flying lessons. In 1928, she was the first woman passenger on a trans-Atlantic flight. Later, she was the first woman to fly the Atlantic alone, the first to fly round-trip to Hawaii, and the first woman to receive the Distinguished Flying Cross. She and her navigator, Fred Noonan, were lost at sea in 1937 near Howland Island while attempting an around-the-world flight in a twin-engine Lockheed Electra. (Lockheed)

NORTHROP AVIATION'S GAMMA was constructed in the 1930s, one of the many expermental aircraft developed in Southern California. The long-bodied Gamma was used by aviation adventurer Lincoln Ellsworth for his Antarctic flight and by Frank Hawks for his non-stop trans-Canada flight in 1933. Developed by Jack Northrop, the Gamma was another step in his efforts to design a plane that consisted of nothing but lifting surface, the flying wing. (Northrop)

[238]

THE NAVY DIRIGIBLE U. S. S. *Los Angeles* settles to its mooring tower. The *Los Angeles* was one of the Navy's picket and anti-submarine airships in service before and during Wordl War II. (NIT)

DONALD W. DOUGLAS (center), founder of Douglas Aircraft and one of the nation's early Southern California aircraft design pioneers, talks business with Engineering Vice President Arthur Raymond (right), and El Segundo plant Chief Engineer Edward Heinemann, shortly before the beginning of World War II. Douglas started his career as a cadet at the U. S. Naval Academy in 1906. He resigned in 1912, and started his studies again from scratch at the Massachusetts Institute of Technology. Despite the institution's belief that it would take him the full four years, he graduated in two. After a short time as a teacher at M.I.T., the young Douglas became chief engineer for airplane builder Glenn L. Martin where he designed the Martin Bomber, an attack weapon that dwarfed all others of its day. Still dissatisfied, however, he packed up his family and started for Southern California to start his aviation empire with total assets of $600. His C-47 Skytrain military transport, its DC-3 civilian counterpart, and his fighter planes, including the Dauntless dive bomber, were some of the most important and famous planes to come out of World War II. (Douglas)

[239]

DR. ALBERT EINSTEIN served as a member of the faculty at the California Institute of Technology in the early 1930s, following his flight from Europe. (Cal Tech)

THE SERRA MUSEUM in San Diego is a classic of Spanish mission architecture The institution, named for Franciscan Friar Junipero Serra who founded many of California's missions, houses many San Diego area historical relics. (SD Title)

COMMUNISTS converged on San Diego on May 30, 1933, in response to rising war tensions in Europe and Asia, and the continuing depression in the United States. The Young Communist League of Los Angeles was denied a parade permit when it refused to guarantee that the red flag would not be carried in the parade. On the appointed day, approximately three hundred Communists converged on San Diego's Memorial park. After railing speeches against President Franklin D. Roosevelt, imperialistic war, and the so-called "boss class," the demonstrators attempted to parade. They were met by a wall of police. In the subsequent riot several officers were injured, approximately thirty demonstrators hurt, eight Communists arrested, and the rest escorted to the city limits. (SD Title)

BUSINESS WAS STILL ACTIVE at the corner of Sixth and Broadway in the San Diego of 1932, despite the Great Depression. (SD Title)

406
BOWLING ON THE BALBOA PARK GREEN was a popular passtime in 1935 San Diego. (SD Title)

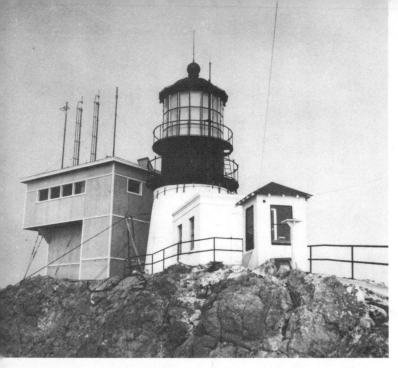

THE FARRALLON ISLAND LIGHT, 89 years after it went into operation, still stood guard over one of the busiest sealanes in the world in 1944. Like most of the more famous lighthouses along the Pacific Coast, the historic old light has been automated in recent years. (USCG)

A HIKER PAUSES FOR A FROSTY DRINK from one of the many streams flowing through the Desolation Valley Primitive Area of Eldorado National Forest in the California mountains near Lake Tahoe. The massive immigration of new residents to the urban centers of coastal California following World War II brought increasing demands for natural recreation areas where urban dwellers could escape from the pressures of their daily lives. (USFS)

The War Years and After: 1940 to the 1950s

CALIFORNIA came of age during this decade. West of California was the war. Shipyards, military camps, Navy bases attracted thousands . . . and after the war many of those who had seen California came back to stay.

California's commitment to the war was total. After the Depression, there were jobs and responsibilities for everyone. Everything, somehow, managed to grow in California in spite of restraints and rationing and shortages. California was the only mainland state shelled by a Japanese submarine, Japanese relocation camp worries started in California, the amphibious war in the Pacific was practiced in California, and California was there with orange juice and movie stars and housing tracts when the fighting forces came home. California was as far east as a lot of the GIs got.

CALIFORNIA NATIONAL GUARDSMEN stand guard on the Golden Gate Bridge immediately after the start of World War II. The state guard was mobilized immediately after the bombing of Pearl Harbor and posted on strategic installations along the West Coast. This particular tower was important to the survival of the bridge because all of the main brace cables were anchored inside it. As the war progressed, men of the California National Guard served in every theater of operations. (CGN)

AMERICAN WARSHIPS bearing the name of California and several of its cities participated in the naval battles of World War II. The cruisers *Los Angeles, San Francisco,* and *San Diego,* along with the aircraft carrier *Monterey,* joined the battleship *California (below)* as commissioned ships of the fleet. The *California,* one of the battlewagons tied up on Pearl Harbor's "battleship row" on December 7, 1941, was sunk at her moorings. She was later reclaimed to take her place again in the van of her fleet. (USN)

STUDENT PILOTS at Mather Army Air Base during World War II stroll along the A.T.6A trainer flight line, as mechanics put the finishing touches on the planes. The California air base revived its pilot-training program during World War II, as well as continuing its navigator training for American pilots. (MAFB)

MATHER ARMY AIR BASE airmen examine the war record painted on the side of the B-29 Superfort bomber "Thumper," as the plane returns from duty in the Pacific in 1945. The base, near Sacramento, became the processing center for most of the B-29s used to reduce the Japanese Empire during the latter days of World War II. Bombers on their way to and from the Pacific theater stopped at Mather for a final checkout before combat or for their first inspection after returning to the United States. (MAFB)

ARMORED TROOPS and Air Corps units trained in the California desert during 1942, learning the tactics they would use during the North African campaign. Camp Irwin has long been the Army's major desert training facility, located as it is in the Mojave Desert. (USASC)

THE S.S. *Robert E. Peary* slides off the ways of the Kaiser shipyard in Richmond during World War II. Kaiser, with a consortium of other companies, built and operated a total of seven shipyards along the West Coast in support of the war effort. The yards revolutionized shipbuilding. The drawn-out procedure of putting a ship together one steel plate and one piece of wiring at a time was abandoned. In its place, round-the-clock building took the form of a ship-assembly line. The spirit of the workers in the yards was one of the most striking phenomena of the war effort. Work gangs frequently broke into song as they went about their tasks. Before the war ended, the yards produced 1,490 ships, including Liberty ships, aircraft carriers, Victory cargo ships, freighters, transports, landing vessels, frigates, and tankers. The *Peary* was started and completed in a total of four days, 15 hours and 26 minutes, a record that still stands for ship construction. (Kaiser)

THE JAPANESE SHELLING of the Ellwood oil refinery near Santa Barbara on February 23, 1942, didn't cause much damage, which is being inspected here by civilian and military officials. A Japanese submarine surfaced off the coast that night and opened fire on the refinery. Although damage was slight, Tokyo newspapers reported a highly successful attack on the American mainland. (SPNB)

TROOPERS of the California National Guard's 40th Division wave their samurai sword war trophies in jubilation as they board trains in Pusan, Korea, for their return home following World War II. (USAC)

STRIKE BREAKER CAMPS filled with fugitives from the Dust Bowl sprang up in Ventura County in 1940 and 1941, when the Teamsters Union led a strike in an effort to organize the Spanish-American workers in the lemon groves. In response to the strike, which dragged on for months, the powerful California Fruit Growers Exchange and other farmer groups hired strike breakers, evicted some of their former workers, and locked some out of the fields. The Teamsters picketed the lemon groves and the few unionized processing plants in the state. In the long run, the union lost the battle, but not before many groves had been damaged from unpicked fruit breaking down trees. (Sunkist)

RIVERSIDE'S MISSION INN remained a peaceful spot during the foment of the 1940s. The luxury hotel was started as an adobe house by Capt. C. C. Miller in 1875. Mrs. Miller used the house to take in boarders, and it developed into one of the early landmarks of the area. Over the years, the inn accumulated a large collection of Spanish and Mexican historical objects. The Saint Francis chapel with its golden Mexican altar and Tiffany windows was built in 1932.

FISHERMEN YANK TUNA ABOARD with hook and line before the days of efficient nets. Tons of tuna were brought back by the San Diego and Los Angeles-based fishing fleets in this manner. The boat would locate a school of tuna, sail into it, and the fishermen would stand along the rail yanking the fish aboard until the school disappeared. (SD Title)

JAPANESE-AMERICANS are rounded up at the Los Angeles railroad station immediately after the start of World War II, for transport into the interior of the nation. The panic following the Japanese strike at Pearl Harbor, and the submarine shelling of a railroad junction in the Santa Barbara area, cast suspicion on all persons of Japanese extraction living along the West Coast. Following the massive round-up, the usually completely patriotic Japanese-Americans spent most of the war in guarded detention camps in eastern Colorado and other Western interior states. Despite the severity of their treatment, from these people came the members of the all Japanese-American 442nd Regimental Combat Team, one of the most highly decorated U. S. Army units in the European theater. (SPNB)

A BLAST FURNACE *(left)* at Kaiser Industries Fontana steel mill was completed in 1942. The first steel production facility on the West Coast, built on what had been a pig farm, was the fulfillment of Henry J. Kaiser's dream of a steel mill near the waterborne shipping of the California coast. At the opening ceremonies *(below),* Kaiser urged American industry to prepare for a switch to peacetime production. Made at a time when there was no end in sight to the fighting, the speech was a shock to most businessmen, but Kaiser had a reputation for thinking well into the future. (Kaiser)

MITCHELL BOMBERS shuffle along a California assembly line on the first leg of their trip along the route their brothers charted to Tokyo in the early days of World War II. The Mitchell was named for aviation advocate Gen. Billy Mitchell, but Lt. Col. Jimmy Doolittle was the man who made the plane famous when his flight of B-25s roared off the flight deck of the aircraft carrier *Hornet* and bombed the capitol of the Japanese Empire in 1942. Nearly 10,000 Mitchells were produced by the California airplane builder. (NAA)

AIRCRAFT DESIGNER Jack Northrop pioneered development of the "flying wing" concept of aircraft design. The Santa Barbara native's early experience was with the Loughead brothers, builders of a twin-engine flying boat. After services in the World War I army and another stint with the flying boat company, Northrop spent four years working up from draftsman to project engineer. It was in 1923 that the young designer got the idea that, since the body of any plane was merely dead weight for the wings to lift, someone should build a plane that was all wing. The Great Depression slowed development of the idea, but the work went forward after Northrop formed his own aircraft company in 1939. With the first Air Force contract in hand, work on the 100-ton all-wing bomber was started in 1942. It continued through the war, but Northrop and his company still had time to build the N-3PB pontoon fighter for the Norwegian government, the P-61 Black Widow night-and-reduced-visibility fighter for the Air Force, and experiment with the installation of rocket engines in the all-wing craft. The planes were delivered to the Air Force in the period between World War II and the Korean War. They taught aero-space engineers many lessons that would be applied in later airborne vehicles. (NIT)

A HUDSON BOMBER bearing the marking of British Commonwealth air forces is rolled out of the Lockheed Aircraft plant in Los Angeles during World War II. Throughout the war, Southern California's aircraft industry rapidly expanded its plants and work force, working around the clock to keep up with the demand for war planes from the United States military and many of the Allies. Although planes were built in other parts of the nation, the American side of the air war had its dominant supply base in Southern California. (Lockheed)

[252]

HOWARD HUGHES' "Spruce Goose" was one of the largest propeller-driven airplanes ever built. The idea for a large amphibian first came to industrialist Henry J. Kaiser during World War II. He reasoned that troops could be moved through the islands of the Pacific by air, thus avoiding the dangers of enemy submarines and long sea crossings. When the War Department accepted the idea, Kaiser brought experienced aviation man Hughes into the project. As it developed, Kaiser withdrew and Hughes became the driving force behind the construction of a large amphibious airplane. When it was ready for public view in 1947, the plane was 218 feet, 6 inches long, had a wing span of 320 feet, and weighed 300,000 pounds. The plane's eight engines each produced 3,000 horsepower, turning propellers that were 17 feet, 2 inches long. The H-4 Hercules flew only once during a trial run in Long Beach. It gained instant attention because the plane was built of wood. After that flight, the Spruce Goose, as it was immediately nicknamed, was returned to its hangar, apparently permanently. (NIT)

AN AIRPLANE-LOAD of movie stars launched the first flight of a Trans World Airlines Lockheed Constellation from Los Angeles in 1946. Included in the passenger list of the first plane were Edward G. Robinson, William Powell, Jack Carson, Walter Pidgeon, Linda Darnell, Celeste Holm, and Virginia Mayo. Early in its history, TWA was under the control of Howard Hughes, who also had control of RKO Studios for a time.

THE HOLLYWOOD CANTEEN was probably the most famous U. S. O. service club in the world during World War II. Crammed with servicemen almost every night, the canteen was manned by volunteers that included some of the most famous movie personalities of the era. (SPNB)

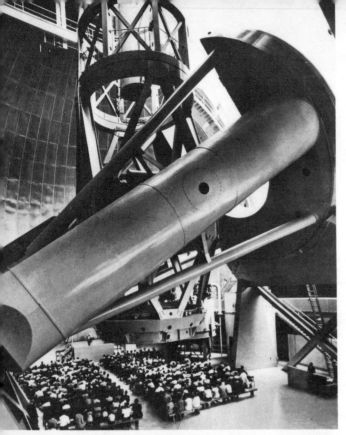

SCIENTISTS AND FRIENDS gather under the huge scaffolding for the 1948 dedication of the 200-inch tall telescope at Palomar Observatory. The observatory was erected on its 720-acre plateau site on Palomar Mountain by the Rockefeller Foundation, for the Carnegie Institution and California Institute of Technology. The lenses for the world's largest eye on the universe were ground in the California Institute of Technology laboratories in Pasadena. (Cal Tech)

THE JET PROPULSION LABORATORY in Pasadena in the early 1940s: A joint effort of the California Institute of Technology and the National Aeronautics and Space Administration, JPL would build the United States' first earth satellites in 1957, would launch the first American satellite, Explorer I, in 1958, and would operate NASA'S deep-space tracking system along with many of the deep-space probes. (Cal Tech)

ONE OF THE RARE SOUTHERN CALIFORNIA SNOWSTORMS does not stop this 1949 Pacific Electric "Red Car" from making its run down Old Mill Road in San Marino.

A FLOTILLA OF PLEASURE BOATS accompanies the cruiser *San Diego* upon its return from World War II, its crew turned out at attention. In the background, hundreds of planes are lined up, mute reminder of the grim business past. (USN)

AN ARABIAN NIGHTS SCENE is reenacted as part of the annual Indio Date Festival.

THE SCRIPPS' MIRAMAR RANCH home just north of San Diego has been preserved as an example of turn-of-the-century Southern California living. The newspaper tycoon was a moving force in San Diego politics until his death in 1926. The *San Diego Sun* was only one of more than thirty newspapers throughout the nation that Scripps controlled from his Miramar ranch home. (SD Title)

PASADENA WENT ALL OUT for the 1946 parade. It was the first since the end of World War II, ending the four-year interruption in the celebration during the war period. Admiral William F. Halsey served as grand marshal of the event. The four tournament presidents who served during the war rode in flower-bedecked cars along with the 1946 president. Theme of the tournament parade that year was "Victory, Unity, and Peace." (Roses)

is one of the more palacial resorts in
California. (UPRR)

PRES. DWIGHT D. EISENHOWER was a frequent visitor
to the El Dorado Country Club golf course in Palm
Springs during his administration.

[257]

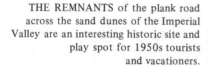

THE REMNANTS of the plank road
across the sand dunes of the Imperial
Valley are an interesting historic site and
play spot for 1950s tourists
and vacationers.

GOV. EARL WARREN and elder statesman Bernard Baruch visit "Baruch's Bench" in the Humbolt redwood groves in 1955. (Redwood)

HAMILTON CITY'S sugar-beet processing plant sits on an island in a sea of beet fields. The industry that got off to such a difficult start in the United States, with several efforts ending in bankruptcy, grew until sugar beets are now grown in almost every area of the California agricultural valley system from the Mexican Border in the Imperial Valley to the Redding area at the northernmost end of the central valley. (Holly)

CARMEL MISSION, founded in the Carmel Valley by Fr. Junipero Serra in 1770, was the prelate's home in California. (MPCC)

SALMON FISHERMEN line Suicide Row when the salmon are running in the mouth of the Klamath River. (Reedwood)

THE GRANDEUR OF DICKS PEAK gains the
attention of a hiker along the Velma Lakes Trail
through the Sierra Nevada in eastern California. The
trail through the mountains is one of the increasingly
popular spots in the Desolation Valley Primitive
Area near Lake Tahoe. (USFS)

THE WORLD'S CROOKEDEST STREET is San Francisco's Lombard Street. The residential street changes
direction ten times in a single block between Hyde and
Leavenworth streets on the eastern slope of Russian
Hill. (SFCVB)

UNION SQUARE is a 2.6-acre grassy haven in San Francisco's shopping district. The column in its center was erected to commerate Admiral Dewey's victory at the Battle of Manila Bay during the Spanish-American War. Pres. William McKinley visted in 1901 to break ground for the monument, and Pres. Theodore Roosevelt dedicated the completed structure in 1903. The park, originally a gift to the city in 1850 from Mayor John White Geary, gained its name from the mass meetings of Union sympathizers held there immediately before the Civil War. During World War II, the grass, trees, and monument were removed for construction of an underground parking garage, and then replaced. (SFCVB)

THE FERRY BUILDING, San Francisco's trademark, hosted up to fifty million travelers before completion of the two bridges spanning San Francisco Bay. The building, erected in 1877 to replace the old Central Terminal Building, extends 661 feet along the waterfront at the foot of Market Street. Its clock tower, 235 feet high and patterned after the Giralda Tower of the cathedral in Sevilla, Spain, was faced in sandstone until the 1906 earthquake shook it off and it was replaced with concrete. The building houses the California State Mining Bureau Mineral Museum and a 600-foot-long relief map of the state with a lighting system that simulates sunrise and sunset and shows volcanic Mount Lassen erupting. (SFCVB)

THE BROWN DERBY restaurant parlayed the shape of its entrance and its famous movie-star clients into a worldwide reputation. (SPNB)

THE 40TH INFANTRY DIVISION of the California National Guard *(above)* parades up San Francisco's Market Street to City Hall after the Korean War in 1954. On the reviewing stand for the return of the division to state control *(below)* were (from left): Gov. Goodwin J. Knight; Gen. Matthew D. Ridgeway, Army chief of staff; W. G. Wyman, Sixth Army commanding general; Acting San Francisco Mayor Mrs. Clarissa McMahon; Maj. Gen. Earle M. Jones, state adjutant general; and Maj. Gen. Homer O. Eaton, Jr., commander of the 40th Division. (CNG)

[263]

[264]

THE UNIVERSITY OF CALIFORNIA was moved from Oakland to Berkeley in 1873, and had a total of 191 students *(above)*. North Hall *(at left)* was demolished in 1917; South Hall has been preserved as a campus landmark. By the mid-twentieth century, the campus *(below)*, had a student body of more than twenty thousand and more than two hundred buildings. It had grown from two buildings in Berkeley to nine campuses granting more than 200,000 degrees. (UCB)

A FARMER *(right)* plows his fields for planting, while another *(above)* uses a mechanical picker to get in the cotton crop. California was one of the first states involved in large-scale corporate farming, and was one of the most important in terms of national agricultural production by mid-1950. With 8,612,702 acres in use, it produced 30,140,900 tons of field crops, fruit, nuts, vegetables, and melons, valued at 1,706,182,000. (CFBF)

THE TRADITIONALLY SLOW, painstaking art of wine making gave way to mechanization in California's vineyards. Large crops of grapes, the potential for larger domestic markets, and the swift growth of American technology affected the wine industry as it did other state agriculture. Here in the mid-1950s, women operate machines that fill wine bottles, cap them, and speed them to shipping containers. (WI)

POINT LOBOS is one of the scenic points along California's Big Sur coast, where rugged beauty is created by the mountains coming right down to the Pacific surf line. Waves along the coast crash against the stone formations, creating strange sculptures in the stone. (CDPR)

THE RUSSIAN CHAPEL at Fort Ross is one of
the remaining relics of early Russian settlement
in California. (CDPR)

INDIAN GEORGE, also known as George Inyo
and George Hanson, was one of the last of the
Death Valley Shoshone Indians still alive at the
time of this 1950 picture. (Evans)

MONTEREY'S FISHING FLEET rides easily at
its moorings between voyages into the northern
Pacific for delicacies.

SUTTER'S MILL *(below)* where James W. Marshall found the nugget that started the 1849 gold rush to California, has been preserved as a historic site for visitors, and a monument *(left)* was erected in his honor. (CDPR)

SUNNY SOUTHERN CALIFORNIA received a spate of heavy rain in 1952 that left deep water in many Los Angeles intersections, such as this miniature flood at the intersection of Slauson and Sepulveda. (CDPW)

SANTA BARBARA'S annual Old Spanish Days Fiesta has long been highlighted by strange and colorful costumes and dancing. (SBCC)

THE PLEASURE BOATS anchored in Long Beach-Los Angeles harbors contrast sharply to the forest of oilwells erected around Signal Hill. (UPRR)

WILLIAM F. BOYD known to generations of American movie fans as Hopalong Cassidy, was one of the celebrities to ride in the 1951 Tournament of Roses Parade. (Roses)

AVIATION RESEARCH kept California in the forefront of technology following World War II. This strange-looking plane, built in Lockheed Aircraft's Burbank plant, was designed for vertical take-offs from Navy aircraft carriers. The XFV-1 was never produced, but it was a step toward future short-takeoff planes. (Lockheed)

MISSILE PRODUCTION on the Nike Ajax assembly line in Santa Monica during the Korean War, as the nation's first practical anti-aircraft missile moves along on hoists to its final stage: Southern California's aircraft industry rapidly became a key factor in the new aero-space business. Rocket Dyne, Edwards Air Force Base, and the Navy's China Lake installations became some of the U. S.'s most important facilities for rocket and exotic aircraft testing. (Douglas, MDC)

URBAN SPRAWL that has made the Los Angeles area world-famous spreads out around the Long Beach Naval Station. Since the population explosion following World War II, Long Beach and Los Angeles have grown to a single urban area. The Navy station is a major West Coast port of the Pacific Fleet. Among the housing tracts are dotted the oil-tank farms spawned by the Signal Hill oil field and the fuel demands of the shipping that passes in and out of Long Beach and Los Angeles. (USN)

MISION DE LOS DOLORES (Mission of the Sorrows) was so well built that it was one of the few buildings that survived the San Francisco 1906 earthquake without significant damage. The basilica was added by Spanish revivalists in 1916. (SFCVB)